GUITAR HEROES

JOHN TOBLER

St. Martin's Press   New York

CONTENTS

Editor: Nicky Hayden
Designer: Chris Lower

Copyright © 1978 by
Marshall Cavendish Limited

Printed in Great Britain

First published in the United States
of America in 1978

Library of Congress Cataloging in Publication Data

Tobler, John.
    Guitar heroes.

    1. Guitarists--Biography. 2. Rock musicians--
Biography. I. Title.
ML399.T65   787'.61'0922 [B]   78-439
ISBN 0-312-35320-0

INTRODUCTION

The world of rock 'n' roll has produced in its comparatively short history a plethora of cult heroes. However, as often as not, their main appeal has not been for their skill and musicianship. Apart, that is, from the great rock guitarists. Here, personality is combined with flair and originality – and it's recognizable to all, no matter what their age or taste.

If it wasn't for the electric guitar, rock 'n' roll probably wouldn't exist. The lead guitarist is the central pivot and energy of most rock groups, so it's not surprising that many have become legends in their own lifetimes. They may (like Jimmy Page) act as complement to a singer, or lead their own bands (like Carlos Santana), or they may even be 'loners', like Eric Clapton and the late Jimi Hendrix. But all have their own following and all acknowledge a debt to the pioneers of the 'fifties and 'sixties.

In *Guitar Heroes* we trace through individual talents the development of the rock guitar, starting with these pioneers – Les Paul (the inventor of the electric guitar), Buddy Holly, Eddie Cochran, Chuck Berry, and others – who wrote the first textbook of rock. Then come the superstars, the dozen, undisputed all-time greats whose recordings and live performances have thrilled millions of fans. Finally come the specialists, names like Jeff Beck, Ry Cooder and the extraordinary Ted Nugent, whose uncompromising attitude and constant experimentation have made them less universally acclaimed but no less influential.

Guitar Heroes singles out the achievements of these legendary figures and places them in the context of the rock 'n' roll movement. Not everyone will agree with our choice – there are always new heroes ready to take their place. But these are the ones that started it all.

Left: Eric Clapton, one of the top three rock guitarists of all time, playing his Gibson guitar at a come-back in London's famous Rainbow Theatre.

PIONEERS

Chuck Berry

Let's begin with the low point of Chuck Berry's career, because after this single catastrophic event, just about everything Chuck has been involved in has been a triumph. In 1959, he was charged with transporting a minor, a fourteen year old Indian girl, over a State line for immoral purposes. The result was a two year prison sentence but fortunately Chuck found himself in 1964 both a free man and a hero.

Charles Edward Berry was born on October 18th, 1931 in St. Louis, Missouri, and began to sing at the age of six in a church choir, and while at school taught himself to play guitar, although he only appeared at school functions. Surprisingly, his influences in terms of singing included Frank Sinatra, but for the guitar were more predictably Muddy Waters, T-Bone Walker, Charlie Christian and the little known Carl Hogan. However, the early Berry style was reportedly almost a night club performance, reminiscent of another of his heroes, Nat 'King' Cole, and this only changed to a more raunchy blues-based approach when Chuck moved to Chicago during the early fifties. While he was there, he played in Muddy Waters' band during early 1955, impressing the veteran bluesman to the point where he recommended that Berry should contact Chess Records for an audition. The result was the release of Chuck's first single, *Maybellene*, in May 1955, which became an immediate American hit, and got to number five in the pop charts. Included among the releases at this time were *Thirty Days, Roll Over Beethoven, Sweet Little Sixteen, Johnny B. Goode, Rock'n'Roll Music, Beautiful Delilah, Little Queenie, Memphis Tennessee* and *Reelin' and Rockin'*, and many more steeped in the tradition started with *Maybellene*.

Chuck's music was a contagious rhythm and blues based rock, featuring exemplary guitar licks and with story lines which instantly appealed to teenagers because of their rebelliousness and in-built humour. Many of his most famous songs centred around the thrill of fast driving, which were accentuated by their rocking beat, and have subsequently become recognized as among the ultimate teenage anthems. Never before had a singer so defined the adrenalin flow produced by being young, and Berry soon became one of the giants of the rock'n'roll movement. He was also granted the accolade of appearing in the celebrated film, *Jazz on a Summer's Day*, a recognition of the fact that he was a superior musician as well as a rock'n'roll showman. In fact, while half his material was the essence of rock'n' roll, the other half was almost completely comprised of slow blues tunes, and a lot of the credit for the reintroduction to popularity of blues artists like Muddy Waters and B. B. King could justifiably be taken by Berry.

At the end of the fifties, the events which led up to his prison term occurred, and Chuck might have easily disappeared into obscurity had not a new generation of British musicians emerged who based much of their musical output on Chuck's early records and those of his label mate at Chess, Bo Diddley. No return to the outside world could have been more fortuitous – the convicted criminal of 1960 turned into the musical hero of 1964.

Chuck soon built on this new found popularity, touring Britain on several occasions and scoring a number of hits like *No Particular Place To Go* and *Little Marie*, which were actually nothing more than fresh lyrics put to the tunes of *Schoolday* and *Memphis*, but his adoring audience didn't care, and Chuck enjoyed his unexpected fame. In 1966, he was made an offer he couldn't refuse by Mercury Records, and spent three years with that company. He then returned to his spiritual home with Chess Records, and began to pick up where he had left off, although his later releases weren't met with any major success until 1972. Then a live recording of a gig in Coventry, England, resulted in a hit single of gigantic proportions and an inverse quantity of subtlety, *My Ding-A-Ling*, which topped the charts on both sides of the Atlantic. This sparked off a further series of reissues of Berry's early classic material, plus another spate of cover versions, which will undoubtedly continue as long as rocks are rolling.

While in recent years Chuck Berry has been a shadow of the man he was during the 'fifties and early 'sixties, his contribution to rock'n'roll has been immense. Possibly no-one else has ever been as influential as Berry was to the various movements he inspired, which included the 'British Invasion', surf music, rhythm & blues and in fact just about every major musical cause since 1960. His stage shows are still capable of filling concert halls all over the world. The most familiar picture of Chuck is one of him performing his famous 'duck walk' (he claims that this most celebrated of rock'n'roll postures was originally designed to hide the creases in a cheap suit) with his cherry red Gibson presented face on to the audience. The model has changed from a Birdland during his pre-jail days to an ES330 or ES335 later, but the sound of Chuck Berry which inspired musicians all over the world has remained essentially the same for twenty years.

Representative albums

Golden Decade   *(Chess)*

Golden Decade Volume 2   *(Chess)*

Golden Decade Volume 3   *(Chess)*

James Burton

Unlike the vast majority of the guitar heroes chosen for this book, James Burton has done very little on his own account, but has made good records into great records for a number of well known artists. It's also fair to say that he remains a particularly private person, and despite the fact that he has influenced and inspired many other musicians, not only guitarists either, what little that is known of the man behind the Telecaster has been revealed almost under protest.

James was born in Shreveport, Louisiana, in 1940, and grew up with country music. His first record was made in 1957, and showed the precocious talents which would continue to decorate rock'n' roll and country records for the next twenty years. Later he joined the cast of a celebrated and very popular country radio show beamed from Shreveport, which was called '*Louisiana Hayride*'. This provided another side to Burton's guitar style, which had previously been dominated by the black music for which Louisiana is famous.

This in turn led to an invitation to play with country star Bob Luman. While rehearsing with Luman at the offices of Imperial Records in Hollywood, Burton was overheard by teenage idol Ricky Nelson, then aged eighteen. Nelson, having scored a couple of big hits and made his debut album, was looking for a backing group to accompany him on the road, and Burton was exactly what Nelson was seeking.

However, it wasn't James Burton's ability as a solo guitarist which was really his major strength, but the extraordinarily tasteful and appropriate way in which he was able to play what are known as fills. A fill is the term used to describe the short instrumental passage usually played to end the verse of a song, or between the lines a singer performs.

Having played on so many hits, it was inevitable that James should become involved in session work, providing backing music for singers who either don't have their own band, or whose own musicians are considered too inexperienced or untalented to make records. A session man's greatest quality is his reliability, not only to appear at the right place at the right time, but also to use his experience to improve a record significantly. Burton could always achieve this.

As Rick Nelson's popularity waned, however the Nelson/Burton partnership folded up, prompted as well by Burton becoming tired of touring, and he was probably encouraged by the money he could now make from sessions. At this point Elvis Presley, who had apparently long coveted James for his own band and now needed a new guitarist, employed Burton for both his recordings and for live work. Apart from the considerable kudos that went with playing for Elvis, his musicians had other advantages. Presley gigs were normally arranged as seasons, playing at the same venue, often in Las Vegas, so that the musicians didn't find it necessary to travel long distances. For Burton, this meant plenty of spare time.

While playing on sessions for Judy Collins, Joni Mitchell, Johnny Cash, the Monkees, and a seemingly endless list of other stars, James made some solo tracks, the two main records resulting being *Corn Pickin' and Slick Slidin'* and *The Guitar Sounds of James Burton*. The former is an instrumental album made with pedal steel guitarist Ralph Mooney in 1967, where country music was fused with interpretations of hits.

Above: James Burton playing at an open-air concert with Emmylou Harris and the Hot Band.

Having worked with the famous, Burton was still prepared to play on the solo albums made by the late Gram Parsons, the man frequently credited with the first successful fusion of rock music and country and western, two musical forms which were previously incompatible. The two albums concerned, *GP* and *Grievous Angel*, featured Burton again on his very top form, as well as introducing to a wide public the golden voice of Emmylou Harris, who sang duets with Parsons. Although the latter died in 1973, the victim of considerable drug abuse, Ms Harris had gained enough interest to make records in her own right, and of course Burton was asked to help.

With the success of the first Emmylou album, *Pieces Of The Sky*, there was a considerable demand for the lady to perform live, particularly in Europe, and perhaps surprisingly, Burton agreed to join her backing group, who were known as The Hot Band. As Emmylou Harris became more popular, it became necessary for James to make the choice between 'The King' and the up and coming artist. It's now history that he chose Presley, justifying his choice by saying that he really preferred to play for him, but of course things might have been different had he known that Presley was about to die.

James Burton is one of the elder statesmen of country rock music, and has been a source of inspiration to almost every guitarist in that field and a large number of players have purchased Fender Telecasters in generally fruitless attempts to imitate the sound of Burton's instrument. As well as the Telecaster, James Burton is a fine dobro player, and in fact is a master of most stringed instruments.

Representative albums

With Rick Nelson	Legendary Masters (*UA*)
	Rick Nelson Country (*MCA*)
With Elvis Presley	On Stage (*RCA*)
With Gram Parsons	GP (*Reprise*)
	Grievous Angel (*Reprise*)
With Emmylou Harris	Pieces Of The Sky (*Reprise*)
	Elite Hotel (*Reprise*)

Eddie Cochran

The enduring memory of Eddie Cochran in most people's minds is of a fairly typical young 'James Dean' type, an 'All-American' boy, tall, dark and handsome, who only looked complete with a guitar slung round his neck. The reality was a little different. Despite his 'moody' image, the real Eddie Cochran wasn't really cast in the James Dean mould, but was ordinary in most ways. Except one – he was a quite brilliant musician, composer and singer.

Eddie was born on October 3rd, 1938 in Albert Lea, Minnesota, the youngest of five children in a family who had been forced to move away from their previous home in Oklahoma City by the Depression. He first began to play the guitar at the age of twelve and was besotted with country and western music, teaching himself to play country hits on his instrument.

In 1953, the family moved again, this time to California, although by this time most of his brothers and sisters had left home, and the young Eddie began to practise very hard on his guitar to combat the resulting solitude, which he hadn't experienced before. This led on to the formation of a small group who played for local functions, and in 1955, he met Jerry Capehart, who later became Eddie's co-writer. Capehart organized Eddie's first recording session, for an almost unknown label, but the single that was released was an instant flop. Capehart and Cochran then began to work making demonstration discs for a publishing company, many of these recordings being commercially released after Eddie's death. They are ample proof that even at the age of sixteen, Eddie Cochran was a guitarist to be reckoned with.

However, he plumped for stardom rather than a steady living, and after releasing another single on a minor label, signed up with the newly-formed Liberty Records. The year was 1957, and Eddie had also been signed up for a cameo part in what has come to be recognized as the finest rock'n'roll film ever made, *The Girl Can't Help It*. Strangely, the song Eddie performed in the film, *Twenty Flight Rock*, wasn't his debut single for Liberty – instead, a John D. Loudermilk song, *Sittin' In The Balcony* was released, and became a hit during May 1957, and was followed up by *Twenty Flight Rock*, which just failed to make the top twenty. Both records have fine guitar breaks by Eddie, who was one of the very few people who played lead guitar on their own records at that time.

Cochran and Capehart came up with a song in March 1958 which finally established Cochran as a top flight star. It was *Summertime Blues*, the only single that Eddie made which went top twenty in both Britain and America. In 1959, *C'Mon Everybody* did nearly as well in America, better in

Britain, and Eddie began to tour on both sides of the Atlantic, developing into as big a live act as he was on record, and proving that he could do on stage everything that he did in the studio.

But by that time, Eddie was looking to the future. He was still making great records, such as *Something Else, Hallelujah I Love Her So, Teenage Heaven, Cut Across Shorty* and several others. But being a rock'n'roll star was not all that Eddie wanted – hit records were desirable, certainly, but by this time he also had a steady girlfriend, Sharon Sheely, and his idea was to settle down in semi-retirement before long.

Unfortunately, that wasn't to be. In early 1960, Eddie embarked on a British tour with Gene Vincent, which went so well that it was extended

Left: Eddie Cochran in classic rock'n'roll pose, as featured in the film 'The Girl Can't Help It'. Below: Cochran as the 'fifties heart throb.

for several months. (George Harrison followed the caravan from city to city, watching Eddie's fingers to memorize the licks.) On April 17th, 1960, he was travelling in a limousine with Gene Vincent and Sharon Sheely, when a tyre burst, and the car ran hard into a lamp post. While Gene and Sharon survived the crash, Eddie sustained multiple head injuries from which he died a few hours later in hospital without regaining consciousness.

Subsequently, Eddie Cochran scored his biggest hit, ironically titled *Three Steps To Heaven*, and a couple of other singles also hit the British charts in the year following his death, *Lonely* and *Weekend*. It's odd that Cochran was so much more popular in Britain than America at the time of his death. It may have been that he perfectly fitted the British idea of the American rock'n'roll star, a novelty in Britain but commonplace in the States – and that this accounted for his lack of recognition in his own country.

Although he was best known as a singer, Eddie's first love was the guitar – once asked what he would do if he lost his voice, he replied 'I'd consider it a blessing!' Unlike most other guitarists of the first rock'n'roll era, Cochran was equally at home with chords and single string solos, and all his best records had a catchy and totally appropriate guitar introduction which made them instantly recognizable. Eddie's chosen guitar was a Gretsch Country Gentleman, and he did a good deal to popularize that model during the late 'fifties and early 'sixties. He was undoubtedly an inspiration to a large number of guitarists who emerged during those years – the fact that his records are still being played as well as being covered by the genuine superstars of the 'seventies says much for their ability to transcend generations.

Representative album

Legendary Masters   *(United Artists)*

Bo Diddley

For a man who in his whole career has only managed to reach the top twenty for one week (at number 20, in October 1959), Bo Diddley has become living proof that you don't need to have hits to be a legend. No doubt he also reflects on the fact that he, along with Chuck Berry, was responsible for the lion's share of the Rolling Stones' repertoire at the start of their career. And they weren't the only ones – the Pretty Things, the Yardbirds, Manfred Mann and many lesser groups all featured Diddley songs, and first found fame while using them.

Bo Diddley isn't his real name, of course. That was Ellas McDaniel, who was born in McComb,

11

Mississippi, on December 30th, 1928, but shortly afterwards moved with his family to Chicago. He started learning the violin at the age of seven, and graduated to guitar before his teens, playing in local clubs, but was unable to make a living out of music. To supplement his income he worked at a large number of unskilled jobs, and also became a boxer for a time, where he acquired the name of Bo Diddley. However, he continued to make music under his real name, although without any real success, until he auditioned in 1955 for Checker Records, a subsidiary of Chess, who had on their books such blues giants as Muddy Waters, Howlin' Wolf, John Lee Hooker and Little Walter.

One of the first records he made was his 'self-dedication', the song *Bo Diddley*. Having previously been a rhythm and blues performer of a somewhat conventional nature, Bo laid down a jungle beat, and the bass-heavy record was quite irresistible to anyone who came within earshot. This hypnotic rhythm became Diddley's trademark, and the record was a major R&B hit, although it didn't feature in the national pop charts. Encouraged by this success, Diddley developed an equally basic stage act, forming a group which contained his half sister, 'The Duchess', on rhythm guitar, plus Jerome Green as full-time maraccas player, later immortalized in another Diddley classic, *Bring It To Jerome*. Another Bo Diddley trademark was the fact that he made his own guitars, which were undoubtedly the most exotic instruments ever used during the period of his rise to fame. His formula was to add a conventional fretboard, usually made by Gretsch, to an unconventionally shaped piece of wood painted in a bright colour. His favourite shapes for these bodies were either square or oblong, although a number of his guitars boasted sweeping curves, or were shaped like equilateral triangles. Bo certainly worked hard to make sure that he was noticed.

But all the visual tricks in the world would have been useless without that distinctive beat. Bo harnessed the rhythm to his fanciful lyrics which cast him in a number of fantastic parts (*Bo Diddley Is A Gunslinger*, *The Greatest Lover In The World*, and *Diddley Daddy* being three representative examples). During this most fruitful period, from 1955 until 1960, Bo wrote and recorded a large number of R&B hits like *Pretty Thing* (from which the Pretty Things took their name), *Roadrunner*, *I'm A Man* (later recorded by the Who), *Say Man* (his one and only top twenty pop hit) and *Who Do You Love*. During those early years, some songs were covered on record, but by the late 'sixties, a positive flood of famous names were featuring them, a particular favourite being *Who Do You Love*, which was recorded by the Doors, Tom Rush and in an astounding twenty minute version by Quicksilver Messenger Service.

The Rolling Stones, strangely have failed to acknowledge their debt to Diddley, recording his songs infrequently. But an early hit, *Not Fade Away*, used the Diddley beat to transform a Buddy Holly B-side into a worldwide smash hit. Even during the seventies, it's not uncommon to hear a group like Dr Feelgood playing a Diddley song, and although the man has now to a great extent lapsed back into the virtual obscurity from which he emerged during the 'fifties, he has left behind a heritage of completely distinctive music which made a great contribution to the rise to fame of many of today's most celebrated groups.

Representative albums

Bo Diddley   London Sessions   *(Chess)*

Golden Decade   *(Chess)*

Duane Eddy

Duane Eddy properly belong with guitarists who are not exceptional in their mastery of the instrument, but whose example as relatively ordinary people had been an inspiration to hundreds of budding musicians. If it's quite plain that the fellow who lives next door to you is no more talented than you are, but has become a star as a result of taking up the guitar, what greater encouragement could there be to attempt a life in music as well?

Duane Eddy was born on April 26th, 1938, in a town called Corning in New York State. His father, also a guitarist, bought Duane a guitar when he was five years old, but the story goes that the boy wasn't very excited about playing it, and hardly touched the instrument for several years. When Duane was thirteen years old, the family moved across the States to Phoenix, Arizona, where Duane first began to hear country and western music, which apparently appealed to him more than any other music. This new found interest in music led Duane to rediscover his guitar which he began to learn seriously. In 1957 he joined a group led by jazz guitarist Al Casey, and also began to take lessons from a noted local jazz guitarist, Jim Wybele.

Around this period Duane also stumbled across the 'sound' which was to make him famous. By turning up the 'reverb' switch on his amplifier, and concentrating on the lower strings of his guitar, he produced grumbling, booming bass-heavy music. He also got to know a local disc jockey

Right: Bo Diddley hammering out his distinctive beat on one of his numerous, outlandish guitars.

named Lee Hazlewood, for whom he occasionally carried out baby sitting chores. Hazlewood produced a few tracks using Duane's songs, which were apparently rearranged. He then sold the finished tapes to Jamie Records of Philadelphia, who immediately signed Duane as an artist, releasing a single of *Movin' 'n' Groovin'* in early 1958. Although it was fairly popular locally, the record wasn't a hit, but later that year *Rebel Rouser* was released, and was a big hit on both sides of the Atlantic, remaining to this day the tune with which Duane Eddy is most easily identified.

Duane's heyday lasted until 1961, when he left Jamie Records. He had achieved another gold record during 1960 with *Because They're Young*, the theme from a film in which he also made his acting debut, and scored hits with *Cannon Ball*, the double sided *Yep/Peter Gunn*, *Forty Miles of Bad Road*, *Some Kinda Earthquake* and *Shazam*. All of these were characterized by a simple guitar phrase first played alone, then as the song progressed, the introduction of the rhythm section, piano and saxophone and finally the voice of a gentleman named Ben De Moto, whose job it was to supply 'rebel yells', allegedly an essential part of the 'Eddy Twangy Guitar Sound'. Duane was also one of the first rock'n'roll artists to make albums which maintained quality throughout rather than the classic 'fifties formula of two hit singles, their B-sides, and eight tracks of low quality uninspired filler. Perhaps the reason why his albums were a better proposition than most was that he used a particularly simple formula which was always successful and it was easy for him to stick to it without changing anything.

Right: Duane Eddy at his height. Below: Buddy Holly with his backing group, the Crickets, and (right) as most people remember him.

In 1962, while still at his peak, Duane signed with RCA Records, and after scoring two hits using the familiar formula, introduced a slightly new sound, where his guitar was set against a female vocal group. Although this was successful initially, and he earned another gold disc for *(Dance With) The Guitar Man*, that was almost his final hit, although he was able to reappear, looking a good deal older, with a remake of *Guitar Man* titled *Play Me Like You Play Your Guitar* in 1975, which briefly reached the British top twenty.

Duane Eddy was the first non-vocal performer to score consistently in the singles chart, and enjoyed a longer run of chart placings than any instrumental act until he was overtaken by the Shadows, whose successes were anyway limited to Britain. Even fifteen years later, Duane remains the most successful solo instrumentalist there has ever been in chart-topping terms, and had it not been for the fact that he is a painfully shy person, his film star good looks might have led him into a career in the cinema. He still plays his guitars – a Gretsch Chet Atkins model for recording, and a Guild Duane Eddy (what else?) for live work, and in 1977 signed a new recording deal with Warner Brothers.

Representative albums

The Legend of Rock   (*Jamie/London*)

Buddy Holly

A measure of the influence of Buddy Holly is that thirteen years after his death, one of his myriad admirers, Don McLean, scored a number one hit with a song about Buddy Holly's death – 'the day the music died' – called *American Pie*. Even more recently, in 1974, Bob Dylan told *Newsweek* 'Buddy Holly and Johnny Ace are just as valid to me today as [they were] then'. Indeed there can be few, if any, musicians from the fifties remembered with such great affection as Buddy Holly.

Charles Hardin Holley was born in Lubbock, Texas, on September 7th, 1936, the son of a tailor. His parents nicknamed him 'Buddy', because he was the youngest of their children, and they felt that his given names, which were tributes to his grandfathers, were a little unwieldy. (His surname was abbreviated to 'Holly', by the way, because his first record contract contained a mis-spelling.) Although his father was not a professional musician, the Holley family were very fond of music, and Buddy's older brothers learned how to play a variety of instruments including guitar, violin and accordion. Despite the family's uncertain finances, musical training was considered essential for all the children, and Buddy began to learn piano at the age of eleven, moving from there to guitar in 1950, when he was thirteen. The music which could be heard around Lubbock was mainly country and western, the traditional sound of Texas, but due to its geographical location, it was also possible to hear Mexican music and blues on the radio with a little dial experimentation. As a result Buddy and his friend Bob Montgomery began to hear blues as played by the three 'Ws' – Muddy Waters, Howlin' Wolf and Little Walter – and this gave Buddy and Bob the edge over their contemporaries who were also interested in music. By 1953, the duo were playing live on the local radio station, KDAV, mingling the odd bit of black music, like *Work With Me Annie* by Hank Ballard and the Midnighters, among the more obvious country

standards. This eventually led to a style which combined the blues and gospel music with country, rockabilly and Mexican influences.

In late 1955, Buddy was invited to make some demonstration tapes for a Nashville talent scout which resulted in him cutting several tracks for the American Decca record company. After a couple of singles had been released unsuccessfully, he was dropped from the label, although subsequently the tracks he cut at that time have been repackaged on more than one occasion. However, his potential was soon afterwards discovered by Coral Records, who put Buddy into the studio with his new-found group, the Crickets. They immediately scored with a top three hit in America which was simultaneously number one in Britain – *That'll Be The Day* – followed by several other big hits. Holly's manager and mentor, Norman Petty, insisted on making records under the name of the Crickets featuring Buddy as lead singer and lead guitarist, but also used the group to back Holly on tracks which would be released as Buddy Holly solos. By this means, while the Crickets continued to score during 1957–8 with *Oh Boy, Maybe Baby* and *Think It Over*, Buddy was simultaneously hitting the charts with *Peggy Sue, Listen To Me, Rave On* and *Early In The Morning*.

Apart from his distinctive vocal style, a mutation of the Hank Williams yodel, and the fact that he had the ability to write simple but unforgettable songs, Buddy Holly was also a very fine guitarist. Once again he was initially influenced by Mexican music, but later also highly impressed by the rockabilly lead played by Scotty Moore, Elvis Presley's first guitarist, and by the blues based rock'n'roll of Chuck Berry and Bo Diddley. During his country and western days, Buddy played a Gibson acoustic guitar, for which he hand-made a leather cover, but when he left Bob Montgomery to join the Crickets, he became one of the first rock'n'roll guitarists to use a Fender Stratocaster, which had first come on the market in 1948 and in Holly's hands became a threat to the previous domination of the Gibson company. Due to his diverse musical influences, Buddy was able to come up with Chuck Berry-like introductions, Bo Diddley rhythms and Scotty Moore fills, making him a guitarist whom many sought to emulate, particularly during the sixties.

Of course, the reason that Buddy wasn't there to experience the tremendous adulation he engendered was that he was tragically killed in an air crash on February 3rd, 1959, along with two other emergent stars, Richie Valens and the Big Bopper. The immediate reaction was that Buddy's then current single, *It Doesn't Matter Any More*, was a big hit on both sides of the Atlantic, staying at number one in Britain for three weeks.

For many artists, the story would have ended there, but the legacy of the three short years of Buddy's recording career seems likely to remain with us indefinitely. His songs have been covered by literally hundreds of artists, from the Beatles to Andrew Gold, from Linda Ronstadt to the Rolling Stones and many others looking for a guaranteed 22-carat song which would give them a great chance of a hit. Tributes in the form of records by his followers have been recorded by Eddie Cochran, Bobby Vee, and several others, including Don McLean's *American Pie*, which we've already mentioned, up to a recent album titled *Holly Days*, by Denny Laine, a member of Paul McCartney's group Wings. McCartney also bought the publishing rights to the majority of Buddy's songs during the mid-seventies, a demonstration of his confidence in Buddy Holly's lasting influence. In the celebrated film *American Graffiti*, one of the characters declared that 'Rock'n'roll's been going downhill ever since Buddy Holly died' – that's never been said of any other popular musician, and probably never will be: Buddy Holly was, literally, irreplaceable.

Representative album

Legend   *(MCA)*

B. B. King

Perhaps one of the most fascinating records held by any of the guitarists in this book is the one attributed to B. B. King, who in 1970 is said to have played to live audiences totalling nearly three million people, apart from the vastly larger television audience who saw him on several 'Specials', one of which was an Ed Sullivan show watched by an estimated seventy million viewers.

Not bad for a kid from a broken home on a plantation in Itta Bena, Indianola, which lies in the Mississippi Delta. That's where Riley B. King was born on September 16th, 1925, but when he was only four years old, his parents split up and Riley was taken by his mother into the fields where she worked. Only five years later the unfortunate lady died, leaving her then nine year old son with no alternative but to continue to work for the plantation bosses. When he was fourteen years old, Riley's father came to find him, but soon afterwards, the Second World War broke out, and at the age of 15, Riley was inducted into the US Army. Just before that he had purchased his first guitar, a red, flat-topped effort which set him back eight dollars. He was taught to play by his uncle, a preacher who accompanied himself in church on the guitar. His army career was brief, for soon after he had completed his basic training, he was ordered back to the plantation he had just left.

He had managed to accumulate a small record collection by this time, and had taught himself how to play by accompanying the recorded sounds of the great bluesmen who had also come from his part of the country, men like Blind Lemon Jefferson and Robert Johnson, as well as the less predictable sounds of Gene Autry, one of the celebrated 'singing cowboys'. When he felt sufficiently adept on the guitar, he began to supplement his income by busking on street corners, and after the war was over, finally moved away from the plantations to Memphis, where he had a cousin, Bukka White, himself a well known guitarist. Here Riley bought his first electric guitar.

Above: B. B. King, the influence for so many younger blues guitarists.

Riley met a harmonica player in Memphis named Rice Miller, who called himself Sonny Boy Williamson II, (the original Sonny Boy having died during the thirties). While playing in 1946 on the *King Biscuit Hour*, the show which Miller hosted, another disc jockey on the station nicknamed Riley 'B.B.', which was short for 'Blues Boy', and since then, Riley B. King has always been known as B. B. King. That 'Blues Boy' tag couldn't have been more appropriate, for the music which B.B. has always played is, of course, the blues, the music which arose naturally out of the deprivation which influenced his early years. In 1949, B.B. signed with a larger record company, Modern, with whom he stayed until the early sixties. This was the period during which his fame was built up.

At this point, B.B. was still to some extent developing his style, which he has described as 'a mixture of people that I've idolized – people like Blind Lemon Jefferson, Robert Johnson, T-Bone Walker, Elmore James and Bukka White'. This stylistic blend seemed to work very well, for one of his earliest sides for Modern, *Three O'Clock Blues*, did well enough to penetrate the national R&B charts in 1950, since which time B.B. has been a regular chart entrant.

During the fifties, B.B. continued to play what is known as the 'chitlin' circuit, a series of ill-appointed small clubs around America which rarely come to the notice of the mainstream of the music business. By the early 'sixties, his longevity had begun to come to the notice of the major record companies, to some extent because of the attention paid to him by better known (and generally white) 'second generation' blues artists, among them Eric Clapton and Mike Bloomfield. By 1963, he was signed to ABC Records, and subsequently a string of successful albums have been released, inevitably showing sophisticated refinements. However, this greater sophistication in no way detracted from the potency of his music, but allowed him to play to wider audiences all over the world, in enormous contrast to the earlier part of his carer. This increase in audience has by no means pulled B.B. away from what he feels are his responsibilities, and during the 'seventies, he has performed at a large number of penal institutions, even recording a live album at Cook County Jail, in addition to his many other commitments. Playing for the under-privileged hasn't prevented B.B. from enjoying the acclaim poured on him by his many white admirers, an example being an occasion during 1968 when a 'superjam' was set up at the Cafe Au GoGo in New York between Eric Clapton, Elvin Bishop and B.B. The white boys went on first and 'each put on a show of flash and dexterity'. When B.B. followed them 'he didn't even stand up. He just sat back in his chair, still relaxing, smiling a little and smoking his Tiparillo, and suddenly he just let go a little pure and ever-so-simple soul, like he'd been doing this for a long time. No fancy playing, just a couple of strokes, and the whole room was wiped out'. Words from Lilian Roxon in her *Rock Encyclopedia*, and most indicative of the man's abilities.

During the 'seventies, B.B. scored his first gold single, *The Thrill Is Gone*, taken from his *Completely Well* album, and has had honors heaped on him from diverse sources. His contribution to the reawakening of black awareness of the music of their heritage, the blues, has been incalculable, and he has helped to bring another fine black artist, singer Bobby Bland, to the notice of the wider audience by recording live albums with him.

As far as guitars go, B.B. complains that a large number have been stolen from him over the years, but remembers with particular affection an original Fender Telecaster, which he used until 1954, when he acquired a Gibson Les Paul. Subsequently he has generally stuck with Gibsons, especially the ES355 stereo model finished in cherry red. However, whichever guitar he uses, B.B. refers to it as 'Lucille', a tradition he started with the purchase of his first electric guitar.

Representative albums

The B.B. King Story Parts 1 & 2   (*Modern/ Blue Horizon*)

Live at the Regal   (*ABC*)

Completely Well   (*ABC*)

Indianola Mississippi Seeds   (*ABC*)

Together, Live . . . For The First Time (with Bobby Bland)   (*ABC*)

Hank B. Marvin

During March 1977, an album made by a group which had broken up nearly ten years before screamed to number one in the British charts, helped along by a television commercial which showed a young lad locking himself in his bedroom, putting on a record, and then watching himself in a mirror as he mimed the guitar parts – using a cricket bat instead of a guitar. He was playing along to the Shadows, who, although almost unknown in America, persuaded thousands of British kids to buy guitars during their years at the top. While the group's rhythm guitarist had his devotees, by far the majority of those bedroom mime artists were pretending to be Hank B. Marvin.

Brian Marvin was born on October 28th, 1941, in Newcastle, and picked up his nickname of Hank because there were a large number of other Brians at his school. His great friend at school was Bruce Welch, and after they had both acquired guitars during their mid-teens, they formed a group called the Railroaders. At this point, Marvin was listening to several jazz guitarists, including Django Reinhardt, Barney Kessel and Wes Montgomery, and also trying to improve his technique via records by classical players, although his main love was rock'n'roll, with particular reference to Buddy Holly, James Burton, Chet Atkins and Bo Diddley. As he told *New Musical Express*, 'It was the rhythm I liked, and the very raw general feel of the sound'. However, the scene in Newcastle was restrictive, to the point where Hank and Bruce decided to venture to London.

When they got to London, the intrepid duo went to the legendary Two I's coffee bar, around which London's first rock'n'roll scene centred after Tommy Steele (Britain's first big-time rock star) had been discovered there. They soon made themselves known there, and within a month of arriving in London were playing regularly (for minimal financial rewards) with a repertoire composed of songs by popular performers of the time, chiefly Elvis Presley, Buddy Holly and the Everly Brothers. By October of the same year, they were on tour with Cliff Richard as his backing group, the Drifters, and although there were several personnel changes in the group, Hank and Bruce continued to back Cliff, Britain's Elvis

Presley substitute, until the mid-sixties.

After Cliff's initial success, it was suggested that the Shadows, as they were now called, should release their own records. After a couple of unsuccessful singles on which Hank and Bruce sang as well as played, the Shadows decided to record a Jerry Lordan song as an instrumental, and within a few weeks, the song, *Apache*, was number one in the British charts, where it remained for six weeks.

This was when the Shadows began to create a huge following in their own right. When they became hitmakers, individual personality cults began to spring up, but Hank's fan appeal was far greater than the rest, no doubt because he was the lead guitarist. Additionally, the Shadows had by accident developed a sound of their own, via a series of effects using an echo box, footpedals and the tremelo arm on Hank's guitar, which at the

Hank B. Marvin, kingpin of the Shadows, showing that style and rock can get together.

time was an Antoria. Hank reckoned that it happened while he was trying to duplicate the sound of American rock'n'roll records, but once found, it became an instantly recognizable and distinctive trademark, and could be heard on twenty hit records between 1960 and 1965, including *Kon-Tiki*, *Wonderful Land*, *Dance On* and *Foottapper*, to name merely those which, like *Apache*, got to number one. Put together with their work behind Cliff, the Shadows' total of hits rises to 63, an amazing number for an instrumental quartet with no pretensions about their own skill.

During their first years together, Cliff Richard decided to buy Hank the guitar of his choice, and Hank, knowing that James Burton used a Fender, got himself a Fender Stratocaster. Later, Marvin and Welch both used Burns-Baldwin guitars, having signed a contract with their manufacturer, but finally found that the Stratocaster suited them better, and Hank has used a Strat, modified by Roka Sound, ever since.

In 1968, the Shadows, who had been inactive for a couple of years, finally broke up, their most successful period behind them. Each of the members then spent more time on production work than anything else. Early in 1977, EMI Records, who had released the Shadows' discs since the start of their career, decided to compile a 20 track album featuring all those more than ten year old hits, which they promoted on television, with the result that after fifteen years, the Shadows achieved their third number one album.

It's difficult to name specifically which guitarists have been influenced by Hank B. Marvin, but it's a fair bet that every British player in this book owes him something. Also, at least one American superstar – Neil Young – freely admits to having been a fan. Rock writer Rex Anderson probably got it right when he wrote, 'I'll tell you how to become a millionaire overnight – all you have to do is persuade every guitarist who admits that Hank Marvin and the Shadows were a great early influence on him to give you a pound'.

Representative album

With the Shadows   20 Golden Greats   (*EMI*)

Les Paul

You'll doubtless notice as you thumb through this book that a particular name keeps reappearing in connection with each person's choice of favourite guitar. Well, maybe it doesn't appear in every case, but a large percentage of our chosen guitarists mention the Gibson Les Paul. Les Paul is not an invented name – he is a real person. In

Right: Les Paul and Mary Ford with the Gibson he made famous, and (far right) together in the studio.

fact he is no less a person than the man who invented the solid bodied electric guitar. Although stylistically a jazz guitarist, an inestimable debt is owed by rock music generally to Les Paul, the man without whom there would be no guitar heroes as we know them.

Lester William Polfus was born on June 9th, 1915, at Waukesha, Wisconsin. He was playing guitar by his early 'teens, his first instrument being a Gene Autry guitar which cost a princely five dollars, after which he used an 'L5', which was probably a Gibson. While still in his mid-teens, he worked out a way in which he could amplify his guitar by sticking a phonograph needle into its body, which then picked up the sound of the guitar in the same way it would have received the sound from a record.

Later, Les persuaded two friends, Jim Atkins (Chet's brother) and Ernie Newton, to travel to New York with him as the Les Paul Trio. He convinced them by pretending he was friendly with the famous band leader Paul Whiteman.

Naturally Whiteman wouldn't speak to him so Les decided to brazen it out and play in the lobby of Whiteman's hotel, where as luck would have it he was seen by Fred Waring, another celebrated band leader, and hired on the spot. That relationship lasted until 1941, when Paul both finished the solid electric guitar he had been working on since the mid-thirties, and left to join Bing Crosby.

As far as the electrification of the guitar went, Paul had been working on different pickups even before he joined Fred Waring, and he finally decided that he could make a guitar with no natural sound source, but with sound produced via pickups and amplification. His first prototype, made in 1941, was known as 'The Log', a piece of wood four feet square with strings, a pickup and a plug. Having found out that by using two pickups a variety of different sounds could be achieved, Paul asked the Gibson company to build him a guitar body capable of holding two pickups. They eventually agreed, but rather than put their name to this outlandish piece of equipment which they considered might damage their good name, they would only allow it to be called the Les Paul Guitar. It wasn't until 1952 that they were prepared to add their name to the model, since when there has been no vast change to this day, apart from technological improvements.

After his stint with Bing Crosby, Paul met and married the singer/guitarist with the Gene Autry Band, one Colleen Summers, whose name he changed to Mary Ford. During the late 'forties and early 'fifties, they are alleged to have scored eleven number ones on the American charts, mostly due to Paul's enormously sophisticated overdubbing methods, which at the time were a considerable novelty. It seemed to those hearing songs like *Mockin' Bird Hill, Lover, How High The Moon, The World Is Waiting For The Sunrise* and *Vaya Con Dios* that there must be dozens of people singing and playing on the records!

Not content with all that, Les had revolutionized disc recording during the 'forties, by building his own recording equipment to a much higher grade specification than had gone before, and also convinced Ampex to build him the very first eight track tape recording machine to his specifications. What else could there possibly be to say about Les Paul? But of course, there's more – like the fact that he developed a guitar pickup which is still the most sought after in the world, and is used on all Les Paul guitars. A story which illustrated the man's incredible single-mindedness, and is absolutely true, is that after a bad car smash in 1948, he was told by doctors that his right arm would have to be set in one position permanently as he had smashed his elbow beyond repair. The medics suggested that perhaps it should be set straight to hang by his side, but Paul would have none of that, and made them set it permanently bent in a guitar playing position!

More recently, Les Paul has returned to performing occasionally, after discovering that there was a great demand for his playing. In particular, he collaborated with Chet Atkins, on *Chester and Lester*, in 1976, while his record company at the time of his hits with Mary Ford also put out *The Very Best Of Les Paul and Mary Ford*, a sixteen track album of their hits.

Even now he hasn't stopped. The latest invention is the 'Les Paulverizer', a sound control system which enables the performer to start and stop tapes by remote control and choose any one of a large number of different sound effects. He will undoubtedly come up with something else very soon . . . and perhaps there is no need to register the fact that the guitar used by Les Paul is, of course, a Gibson Les Paul!

Link Wray, creator of the legendary 'Rumble', on tour recently with Robert Gordon.

Representative albums

The Very Best of Les Paul   *(Capitol)*
and Mary Ford

Les Paul Now!   *(London/Decca)*

Chester and Lester (with Chet Atkins)   *(RCA)*

Link Wray

During 1971, Pete Townshend of the Who was working in the Record Plant Studio in New York, when Link Wray walked in. After brief introductions, Townshend allegedly knelt down in front of Wray, and bowed deeply, saying 'This is the King. If it hadn't been for Link Wray and "Rumble", I never would have picked up a guitar'.

Lincoln Wray was born on May 2nd, 1930, in Fort Bragg, North Carolina, in the Appalachian Mountain region. His great grandmother was a full blodded Shawnee Indian, a heritage which shows clearly in his facial structure, but his parents were both considered as white people. Despite this, Link still had to attend the Indian

school, as segregation was still strongly practised in that area.

Encouraged by his mother, Link learned to play guitar with an instrument which cost four dollars, and is said to have started to play in public in 1942 with a group he organized from among his family and friends who played 'standard' pop songs like *Deep Purple* and *Stardust,* together with country music appropriate to the area where the Wray family lived. Still during his teenage years, Link was strongly influenced by a black bluesman named Hambone, who taught him to play in open tunings (often used by ethnic blues players), and also demonstrated a bottleneck effect which could be obtained with a knife.

After this, Wray was called up and served in the Korean war, where he later contracted tuberculosis. As a result, he was hospitalized for a year and lost a lung. After recovering from this illness, Link returned to music, apparently after seeing Bill Haley and the Comets perform locally. Having previously concentrated on singing, Wray became more interested in the possibilities of the lead guitar, and during the early fifties wrote *Rumble,* the song upon which his legendary status was originally based. A demonstration version of the song was played on a Washington radio station, and after some negotiation, the very successful Cadence label.

Rumble was a guitar-dominated instrumental, and featured sounds which had never been heard before, the tremolo, the fuzz tone and a wah wah effect, all staples of today's rock guitar sounds. The fuzz tone was achieved by making small holes in the guitar's loudspeaker, while the wah wah effect was the result of Link's use of what must have certainly been the first voice box, a tube leading from the speaker to his mouth.

Eventually, *Rumble* achieved sales of a million and a half, being certified 'gold' some four years after it was first released. However, Link was not prepared to conform to the wishes of the various record companies who signed him during the 'fifties and 'sixties, feeling inhibited by the artificiality of the normal studio situation. As he later put it, he played 'honest music', and recording in over-sophisticated surroundings in places where he felt a stranger was not, in his terms, 'honest'. As a result, the only notable record he made between *Rumble* in 1954 and his more recent comeback in 1971 was a track called *Rawhide,* which also achieved gold record status in 1959. However, Wray did make two extremely obscure albums during this lengthy period, *Link Wray and the Raymen,* released, like *Rawhide,* via Epic Records in 1963, and *Jack The Ripper* titled after a near-hit, which came out on Swan Records.

During the late sixties, Link Wray moved with his family to a farm in Accokeek, Maryland, and eventually converted a disused chicken coop into a makeshift studio, installing his brother Vernon's three track tape recorder. In this building, which became known as 'Wray's Shack Three Track', Link and his associates began to record for their own amusement, and also played successful gigs locally. At one of these appearances, Steve Verroca was in the audience. Verroca was an independent producer, and persuaded Link to try his luck again as a recording artist, eventually sealing a deal with Polydor, although considerable interest was also shown by the Beatles' Apple label at the instigation of George Harrison. On this 'comeback' album, released in 1971 and simply titled *Link Wray,* Link not only played guitar, bass and dobro, but also sang.

Around this time, a compilation album was released of a number of the tracks Link had made during the 'fifties and 'sixties under the title *There's Good Rockin' Tonight,* and since then, four more albums have been released, variously on the Polydor and Virgin labels. During the 'seventies it has been claimed that among those guitarists who revered the name of Link Wray, and were strongly influenced by him, are Townshend, Harrison, Jimi Hendrix and Frank Zappa and he is considered by many to have been ten years ahead of his time when he first emerged as an artist. A critic at the time of his rediscovery made a parallel between Link and the 'no holds barred' sounds of the Who and the Yardbirds at the time of their emergence, and undoubtedly his earthy and often bluesy style is reflected in many of today's superstar guitarists. For the major part of his career, Link's preferred instrument has been a Gibson guitar manufactured in 1910, its age being reflected in its primitive shape, and thus it has been particularly difficult for others to reproduce the sound he achieves. However, he also plays a variety of more modern guitars, both electric and acoustic, made by several manufacturers including Fender and Gibson, using a Gibson Les Paul more than most of the others. 1977 saw him featured on a rock'n'roll revival album made by a very promising singer from Washington, Robert Gordon. As a result of this connection he has been offered his own recording deal by Gordon's label, Private Stock. As a result, Link Wray's legendary talent is, at last, being appreciated by an ever-increasing audience.

Representative albums

There's Good Rockin' Tonight   (*Union Pacific*)

Link Wray   (*Polydor*)

Beans and Fatback   (*Virgin*)

Robert Gordon with Link Wray   (*Private Stock*)

23

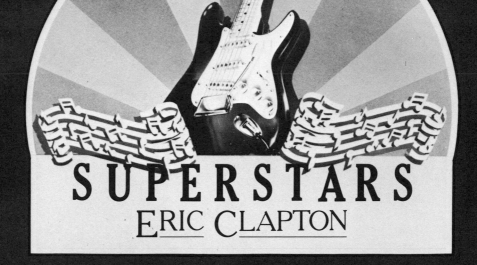

SUPERSTARS
ERIC CLAPTON

Around 1965, the first signs began to appear on disused buildings. 'Clapton is God', they said, and to a certain element of the youth culture of that exciting period when British music was where it was at, the sentiment, while obviously absurdly exaggerated, was remarkably close to the truth. Eric Clapton, at that time the guitarist with John Mayall's Bluesbreakers, was the hottest thing around in guitar terms, attracting a totally besotted and predominanetly male audience who swooned to his every note.

Eric Clapton was born on March 30th, 1945, the son of a bricklayer, at Ripley in Surrey. By the time he left school, he had decided to become a designer of stained glass, attending Kingston College of Art for the purpose. During his early teens he had been given a cheap guitar by his parents which he briefly played and then forgot about. However, Kingston was in the 'Thames delta', the home of the British rhythm and blues

boom, which spawned such world famous groups as the Rolling Stones and Fleetwood Mac, to mention only two of the groups who moved on to bigger things after starting in the area. Almost inevitably, Eric became involved with the music which surrounded him, being particularly attracted to the blues, a music form which tends to stress the hardships of life, with which Eric, as a student, could easily identify. Discovering that many of his acquaintances were earning money by making music, he picked up his guitar again, and by the time he was asked to leave the Art School, was playing it at every available moment.

The first genuine group with whom he was involved was called the Roosters, which existed during 1963. Tom McGuiness, later in the Manfred Mann group and McGuiness-Flint, was the only other notable name in the band, and when the Roosters folded up in the autumn of '63, he and Eric joined Casey Jones and the Engineers, playing behind Jones, a Liverpudlian who had made a single and needed a backing group to help him promote it. In fact, Eric only stayed a couple of weeks with the Engineers – being a blues purist strongly influenced by blues players from America like Freddy King, Otis Rush, Muddy Waters and Big Bill Broonzy, he found the 'pop' aspect of the band too much to take.

Almost immediately, he stepped into the Yardbirds, whose original guitarist Top Topham had decided to give up professional playing. While he had attracted some small attention with the Roosters and the Engineers, it was during his eighteen month stint with the Yardbirds that Clapton really began to be noticed. The █████ were fortunate enough to follow the Rolling Stones into a Sunday night residency at one of the most famous clubs of the era, the Crawdaddy, and the enormous audience which the Stones had nurtured over the previous year were quite ready to accept the Yardbirds as the replacement for Jagger and co., who were on the verge of their first hit and fast becoming inaccessible.

At the end of 1963, the Yardbirds made their first record, acting as the backup band for ⸱ legendary American harmonica player Sonny Boy Williamson, who was by then well past his best, but whose status as 'the real thing' in blues terms made it a very prestigious gig for the group. Doubtless Clapton was both pleased by Williamson's demonstrative recognition of his talent, but simultaneously embarrassed by the obvious decline of his hero's prowess. Soon afterwards, the Yardbirds began to reject their ethnic roots, opting instead for a more rock oriented direction which Clapton, remaining a purist, was unwilling to condone. Thus, despite the fact that he played on the group's first hit *For Your Love*, which reached the top ten on both side of the Atlantic, Eric decided to leave the Yardbirds in March 1965.

Eric's next band was John Mayall's Bluesbreakers. Before he joined, they were already attracting a strong following around Britain, but by the time he eventually left the group, they had become an enormous attraction, and Clapton the most widely acclaimed guitarist in Europe, if not the world. Apart from their incredibly exciting live gigs, the basis for much of the band's popularity was an album titled *Bluesbreakers*, which continues to sell in quantity twelve years after it was released.

He didn't stay long. Mid-1966 saw the formation of Cream, perhaps one of the very few supergroups who genuinely deserved the name. Along with Jack Bruce on bass and Ginger Baker on drums, Eric reached heights of popularity exceeded only during that period by the Stones and the Beatles. Cream's music still had an undeniable touch of blues in it but the trio format allowed Clapton to lift off into areas of music which would never have been possible in the Mayall band, although ironically they were areas not dissimilar from those covered by the Yardbirds. Heavily amplified, with ample opportunity for rock-oriented guitar solos sometimes lasting several minutes, Cream were together from July 1966 until November 1968. They released four highly successful albums, including a double LP – *Wheels of Fire* – half of which was made in the studio and the other half recorded live. This latter half perhaps demonstrated where the strength of the group really lay. It was also the

reason why Cream broke up at the height of their popularity, when the individual members of the group found it impossible to withstand the strain that constant touring and great fame was exerting on them. Subsequently, five other albums of their work have been released, taking in live cuts, odd singles and various compilations.

Despite the fact that the formula behind Cream had presented problems as well as fame, a similar blueprint applied to the next Clapton venture. The group involved was Blind Faith, on paper at least even more of a supergroup than Cream, but nevertheless a patently manufactured combination, with Eric and Ginger Baker from Cream, Steve Winwood from Traffic, and Rick Grech from Family. In this combination one album was recorded which sold well despite its shortcomings. The group also played their first live date in front of a huge crowd at a free concert in Hyde Park.

In January 1970, the group found it impossible to stay together any longer due to both business pressures and personal incompatability, but before the final farewells, Eric flew to Toronto in Canada, to appear with John Lennon of the Beatles in a 'concert for peace', the somewhat patchy results of which are preserved on an album released on the Apple label. Perhaps the spontaneity of that occasion appealed to Clapton, being a direct contrast to the two previous groups with which he had been involved, both of which had seemed to expect him to produce innovative bursts of guitar with great rapidity and frequency. His next venture after the one-off gig with Lennon was to travel around Britain and Europe with Delaney and Bonnie (Bramlett) and Friends, a free-blowing, gospel tinged rhythm and blues/soul group, which contained many of today█████p session players, although at the time they were virtual unknowns. Clapton's enthusiasm for the project was such that no less a person than George Harrison, a friend from the days of Cream, also helped out on some of the gigs, and a live album was released with the unwieldy title of *Delaney and Bonnie and Friends On Tour With Eric Clapton*.

When the tour ended in March 1970, Eric went to Los Angeles to finish his first solo LP, which had been started during the latter days of Blind Faith. When it was released, it seemed to indicate a rather confused Clapton, who by this time had become involved with heroin, the drug which nearly put an end to his career by the middle 'seventies. But before he virtually vanished from the scene. Eric put together an astonishing four piece band, Derek and the Dominos, which further fused the blues and rock styles which Clapton by this time had made on his own. Derek and the Dominos (the name was designed to take █ the pressure off Clapton by not mentioning his name) put out a double album at the end of 1970, which many feel contains Clapton's finest work. The album was called *Layla*, and the title track was released as a single which still rates as one of many people's top ten singles of all time. The highlight of this particular track was the magnificent guitar playing of Clapton and Duane Allman, playing as if their lives depended on it – and maybe they did, for Eric was extremely ill due to his drug problems, and Duane was dead less than a year later, killed in a motorcycle accident.

The Dominos fell apart in just under a year, and Clapton did very little for nearly two years, with the exception of one remarkable event which took place in August 1971. That was the celebrated Bangladesh concert presented in New York, and organized by George Harrison in an attempt to assist the starving millions there.

At that point, Eric Clapton left the limelight, becoming steadily more introverted as a result of his addiction. It wasn't until January 13th, 1973, that he appeared on stage again, in a comeback concert at London's Rainbow Theatre specially arranged for him by Pete Townshend of the Who. Almost inevitably, the concert was recorded. A year and a bit later, now almost completely cured of his addiction by acupuncture treatment, Eric formed the simply titled Eric Clapton Band in April 1974, and since that time, he has gradually recovered his previous mastery of the guitar, retrieving much of the popularity he enjoyed with Cream, and seems likely to exceed it in the near future, judging by the tremendously acclaimed live appearances and the annual album released each year since 1974.

Eric Clapton has played a variety of guitars during his career, but his favourite remains a Fender Stratocaster. Apparently, Clapton first saw a Strat being played by Buddy Holly whereupon he exclaimed 'What is that space vehicle?', and acquired one for himself as soon as he could. He also uses Gibson guitars at various times, among a proliferation of guitars which he owns.

REPRESENTATIVE ALBUMS

John Mayall's Bluesbreakers   Bluesbreakers
                                   (London/Decca)

Cream   Wheels of Fire   *(Atlantic/Polydor)*

Derek and the Dominos   Layla
                             (Atlantic/Polydor)

Eric Clapton   461 Ocean Boulevard   *(RSO)*
                    E.C. Was Here   *(RSO)*
                    Slow Hand   *(RSO)*

PETER FRAMPTON

Although the vast majority of the record buying public may think that Peter Frampton is one of the newer names in rock music, he is actually a supreme example of the way in which persistence can eventually lead to stardom. When, in 1976, his remarkable double album *Frampton Comes Alive* topped the American album charts for an unprecedented seventeen weeks, finally becoming the biggest selling double album of all time, it was the reward for twelve years of toil in the music business, and at least three near misses in the arduous struggle to become a star.

Peter Frampton was born on April 22, 1950, at Bromley in Kent, a few miles south-east of London, and is the son of a musician. His father never achieved huge fame, although he was a member of a number of jazz groups and dance bands, but certainly put Peter on the same road by giving him a guitar at an early age, and by exposing him to the incomparable guitar music of the French gypsy, Django Reinhardt. Even now, one of Peter's all-time favourite pieces of music is Reinhardt's *Nuages*, and the first record he ever owned was also by Django. Frampton's first group was known as the Preachers, and was composed of young local musicians, although he had been in a less serious band at school called the Truebeats, who specialized in copying the work of the Shadows and the Ventures. With the Preachers, who were managed by Rolling Stone Bill Wyman, Frampton first went into a recording studio, although the results (engineered incidentally by Glyn Johns, who later found fame working with the Rolling Stones, the Eagles and Steve Miller) were never released.

After the break up of the Preachers, it was time to choose between studying music at college or joining a group. By this time, Peter had

investigated several types of music, from the early jazz stylings of Django through the pop/rock sounds of Hank B. Marvin and the Shadows to the more melodic sounds of jazz guitarists like Kenny Burrell, who played with organist Jimmy Smith, and Wes Montgomery. Despite this bias towards jazz, the thought of becoming a pop star appealed to Peter so much that he decided to forgo college, and instead joined the Herd, another local group, but a highly respected one. The Herd was an almost instant success, a teeny-bopper band playing music which was somewhat lacking in adventure, but which was most successful during 1967–8, scoring three British hit singles within eight months, the best remembered of which is *From the Underworld*. All four members of the Herd sang as well as playing their instruments, but Peter, because of his good looks, was singled out for particular attention, and dubbed in one British music paper as 'the Face of '68'.

Despite their promising start, the Herd, like many other young groups both before and since, were insufficiently acquainted with the ways of the music business, and found that a large number of people connected with the band were doing rather better out of it than the musicians themselves, the result being that the band broke up in disarray during 1968. Frampton had discovered during his time with the Herd that less and less attention was being paid to his guitar playing, while his image as a teen idol was becoming ever more potent. Having previously come across David Bowie at the local Beckenham Arts Lab, and finding more interest in such experimental work than in straight pop, Frampton determined to join a group where his musical abilities would not be secondary to his looks.

Steve Marriott was a friend from the days when

both he and Frampton were members of hitmaking groups, Marriott's being the Small Faces. With a distaste for instant but fickle stardom in common, the two began to jam together at Marriott's home. Marriott first of all introduced Frampton to drummer Jerry Shirley, and soon decided that he had been with the Small Faces long enough himself. So Humble Pie was born, completed by bass player Greg Ridley from Spooky Tooth. During its early days, Humble Pie was a predominantly tasteful group, who produced several well thought out albums without really achieving as much commercial success as their record company might have liked. A change in direction was decreed, and from the initial co-operative concept of 'front man' duties being shared, Steve Marriott began to emerge as leader of the band, probably due to the predominance of heavy rock which they played. After the group's fifth album *Performance – Rockin' the Fillmore*, (a double live album recorded in New York and their most successful up to that point), Frampton decided it was time to leave.

For the next few months, he became involved strongly in the session scene, and quickly became an in-demand studio guitarist, helping out on records by George Harrison, John Entwistle, Nilsson and Nicky Hopkins. At the same time, he was turning over future plans in his mind prior to making his first solo album, which eventually emerged in 1972 under the title *Wind of Change*. Peter had stockpiled a lot of ideas during his work with both the Herd and Humble Pie, and was able to show the width of his eclecticism from acoustic ballads to hard rocking work-outs, like his rearrangement of *Jumping Jack Flash*. He also took the opportunity to demonstrate that the guitar, although perhaps his favourite instrument, was just one of several at which he was adept. A group was eventually formed to play on the road under the name of Frampton's Camel. After touring extensively and almost exclusively in America, the group made an album simply titled *Frampton's Camel*, much more of a hard rock album than its predecessor, but soon after it was released, the group reverted to the simpler name of Peter Frampton, also going through a certain number of personnel changes. By the time he was ready to make his third LP, Peter had decided to take over nearly all the keyboard duties for the band in addition to guitar, thus reverting to the formula used on his first album.

Regrettably, the pattern didn't change significantly for the 1975 album, *Frampton*, which had slightly different personnel. It was as if Peter was searching somewhat desperately for the correct formula, but once again the result wasn't very different from what had gone before, although a couple of songs were included which were destined to become world-famous a year later. A fairly permanent backing group now surrounded Frampton, the nucleus of which was made up of Andy Bown, ironically an ex-member of the Herd, on bass, and John Siomos on drums. Both had been on previous Frampton albums, although never previously together.

1976 was the year when it all happened for Peter Frampton. It wasn't that his music had significantly improved or even changed since the first solo record four years before, but perhaps the world had caught up with him. Whatever the reason, the 1976 Frampton LP, a live double album titled *Frampton Comes Alive*, captured the imagination of the American public, and dominated the album charts to become the largest selling live LP of all time, despite the fact that it was a double. It also provided Peter with his first solo success in Britain, where he played live to an adoring audience for the first time in several years. On both sides of the Atlantic there were three single hits, *Show Me the Way* and *Baby I Love Your Way*, both of which had previously appeared on the *Frampton* album without attracting too much notice, and *Do You Feel Like We Do*, which went back even further, to the *Frampton's Camel* record. This double album finally established Peter, after more than twelve years of trying, as a genuine gilt-edged rock star, with his twin advantages of inspired musicianship and good looks finally complementing each other rather than getting in each other's way, and the position was further consolidated by his 1977 album, which was titled *I'm In You*.

Only now is Peter's huge ability as a guitarist being recognized for what it is, and a certain amount of the credit should go to his guitar. Until his latter days with Humble Pie, Peter found it difficult to choose an appropriate instrument, but he was given a 1954 model Gibson Les Paul when the band were playing in San Francisco, which has remained his favourite ever since. Its previous owner had to a certain extent customized the instrument, shaving the neck and revamping the body as well as adding a third pick up. Peter also uses a twelve string guitar made by Ovation but mainly for recording purposes, plus a Gibson Melody Maker and a Martin D45 acoustic.

REPRESENTATIVE ALBUMS

Humble Pie   Performance – Rockin'
                The Fillmore (*A&M*)

Peter Frampton   Frampton Comes Alive   (*A&M*)

Peter Frampton comes alive to an audience who can appreciate his playing as well as his good looks.

GEORGE HARRISON

If you don't know who the Beatles are, or at least were, there's a good chance that you must have just landed from another planet. Perhaps there's a little more excuse for not being quite sure of George Harrison's contribution to the Beatles' success, because he was always the most self effacing member of the group, although his musical ability as a player probably exceeded that of any of the others.

George was born on February 25th, 1943 in Wavertree, Liverpool, and his early years were spent in an exceedingly normal way. When he was thirteen years old, he bought a cheap guitar from a school friend, and taught himself how to play, soon afterwards replacing this original instrument with a £45 electric model. During that same year of 1956, George played in public for the first time, and also renewed his friendship with another schoolmate, Paul McCartney. Together, they began to play the songs of Lonnie Donegan, who was very popular at the time, and soon afterwards, both Harrison and McCartney joined the Quarrymen, a group led by John Lennon. Of course, it was a strictly amateur group, and when George left school in the summer of 1959, he had to find himself a job, and for some time worked as an apprentice electrician in a store in Liverpool.

By 1960, the three future Beatles-to-be had changed the name of the group to the Moondogs, and later became the Silver Beatles, with George, a great fan of rockabilly star Carl Perkins, changing his name briefly to Carl Harrison. During this period, the music that he was playing was predominantly unoriginal, but George was learning his trade, and his guitar style was strongly influenced by American rock'n'roll artists like Perkins, Buddy Holly and Chuck Berry, whose songs were a major part of the group's repertoire. Later that same year, the group, by now called simply the Beatles, served the apprenticeship which has become a romantic part of their legend – playing eight hours a night in unpleasant clubs in Hamburg, Germany. George, however, the youngest member of the group, was deported from Germany for being under age and the Beatles had to wait until his eighteenth birthday before they could return to Hamburg. During the next year and a half the foundations were laid for what was to be an earth-shattering career. During that period, Ringo Starr joined the group, they met their manager to be, Brian Epstein, and after being turned down by a number of record labels, were taken on by George Martin, who signed them to EMI's Parlophone label. Subsequently, the various well-known events occurred which made the Beatles the most famous group the world is ever likely to see.

In 1966, George's attention turned eastward to India, visiting that country to soak up its atmosphere at first hand and also taking lessons on the sitar, the highly complex 'guitar of India', from Ravi Shankar, the man generally considered as being its major practitioner.

Up to this point, George had been very much a minor league songwriter, dwarfed in the shadow of John Lennon and Paul McCartney, but on the Beatles' *Sergeant Pepper's Lonely Hearts Club Band* album, the Harrisong (also the name of George's publishing company) was an Indian-style opus titled *Within You, Without You*, which probably for the first time focussed public attention on this third songwriting Beatle – although not necessarily because the song was a masterpiece, but more likely because of its strong contrast with the Lennon/McCartney compositions elsewhere on the album. George, like many other

show business personalities also became strongly involved in Transcendental Meditation, as practised and taught by the celebrated Maharishi Mahesh Yogi. While others lost interest, India continued to hold a fascination for George, and since the time when he worked there on the musical score for the film *Wonderwall* in 1968, a portion of his musical output has always been influenced by that country.

When the Beatles started their own record company, Apple, an immediate project was to record Jackie Lomax, another Liverpudlian, who had travelled a similar but far less successful road to George. Harrison produced Lomax's LP *Is This What You Want?* and also contributed the song generally felt to be the high point of the record, *Sour Milk Sea*. With more time to spend on writing, George also quickly improved as a songsmith, coming up with four memorable songs for what is known as the Beatles' 'White' album, the best of which is *While My Guitar Gently Weeps*, the recording of which is a feast of rock'n'roll guitar at its best, featuring George and also Eric Clapton. Similar activities continued through 1968–9, but with most of George's time taken up by production.

George Harrison (right) taking a typically modest back seat to Delaney Bramlett (left) and Eric Clapton, on tour in the UK in 1969.

By the end of 1969, more than three years after the Beatles had performed in public for the last time, George got the bug to be on the road again, and attached himself to the British tour undertaken by Delaney and Bonnie and Friends, the American white soul circus which featured so many of the top session musicians of the 'seventies, but who were then next to unknown. He wasn't the only English guest with the groups, as both his friend Eric Clapton and Dave Mason, who had left Traffic not long before, were also in attendance.

1970 saw George Harrison really break out of his role as 'the guitarist with the Beatles'. Much of the year was spent writing and recording his first solo project, the magnificent triple album *All Things Must Pass*. As well as playing some fine guitar, George also proved that he was no mean singer, and could write songs as commercial as his ex-colleagues, a case in point being his devotional anthem *My Sweet Lord*, which reached the top of the singles charts in both Britain and America.

Any feelings of anti-climax were soon eroded by the event for which George Harrison will probably be most remembered, an all-star concert he organized to help the starving millions in the breakaway Indian state of Bangladesh. At a few days notice, a bill was organized which included Bob Dylan, Leon Russell, Billy Preston, Eric Clapton and Ringo Starr among others, and was led by George himself and Ravi Shankar. They played two concerts at New York's Madison Square Garden, which were filmed, and yet another triple album was later released. Apart from the fact that the concert marked the first public appearance by Bob Dylan for some considerable time (he and George had collaborated as writers on *I'd Have You Anytime* on *All Things Must Pass*), the concert saw the return to the stage of Eric Clapton, who once again worked magic with George on a sizzling version of *While My Guitar Gently Weeps*. The relationship between the two aces had continued since 1969, when George had guested under the pseudonym 'L'Angelo Mysterioso' on *Badge*, one of the final tracks recorded by Cream. 1972 was a quiet year for George following the efforts of the previous twelve months, and it wasn't until mid-1973 that another solo album, *Living In The Material World*, was released. Also around this time, George decided to start his own record company, Dark Horse, and the first artists on it, the Shankar Family and Friends, and the English soft rock duo Splinter, were both produced by George, who also toured during 1974 with his Indian friends, but to a decidedly mixed reception.

Since then, a number of George Harrison albums have been released, including *Extra Texture, Dark Horse* and *33⅓*, but none of them has approached the success of the two earlier triple albums, either artistically or commercially. However, George seems happy enough with the various other projects he is involved in, which now include films as well as record production, and during the latter half of the seventies, he has not apparently been involved in the musical innovation which marked his Beatle years.

As a guitarist, George Harrison is rarely considered in the same breath as some of his contemporaries like Eric Clapton. However, like several of the artists who originally influenced him, he has been the inspiration for large numbers of guitarists. Additionally, his trail blazing work in bringing an Indian influence to popular music may never be gauged, and his early pioneering work in searching out exotic stringed instruments (and learning how to play them), has opened the doors for many innovatory musicians. It is, after all, very easy when you're a member of a group like the Beatles to allow your musical ambition to stagnate but George Harrison has never allowed this to happen, and while silence surrounds his work during the late 'seventies, it is more than likely that he is striving once again to widen and improve his musical knowledge.

While he has never been an extended soloist, a number of George's guitar passages are instantly recognizable, such as those in *Something, My Sweet Lord, Here Comes The Sun* and the frequently mentioned *While My Guitar Gently Weeps*. It should be noted that this dearth of solo activity is not due to lack of ability, but the fact that the major part of his early work was involved with pop, rather than rock music. Several fine examples of this most praiseworthy sparseness can be heard on a compilation which includes his work both as a Beatle and later as a solo artist, *The Best of George Harrison*. In terms of style, traces inevitably remain of those early rock'n'roll influences, but since leaving the Beatles, George has become simply a highly creditable rock guitarist. His favourite and most prized guitar is a 1956 Fender Stratocaster, although he of course possesses a number of other stringed instruments, including several sitars.

REPRESENTATIVE ALBUMS

The Beatles 1962–1966	*(Apple)*
The Beatles 1967–1970	*(Apple)*
All Things Must Pass	*(Apple)*
The Concert For Bangla Desh	*(Apple)*
The Best of George Harrison	*(Parlophone)*

JIMI HENDRIX

The one player in this book who needs no introduction is Jimi Hendrix. From the moment he appeared for the first time in Britain at the end of 1966, Hendrix grasped the imagination of rock fans throught the world. During his brief but glorious time at the very top of the superstar tree, he was a continual source of inspiration, not just to guitarists, but to musicians of all types, and even to non-musicians, who could see in him something unique – a person who was entirely his own man, and was much more a leader than a follower. How many others could justify such a claim?

James Marshall Hendrix was born in Seattle, Washington on November 27th, 1942, the son of a landscape gardener. His childhood might be described as turbulent – his parents were apparently prone to disagreement, and the young Jimi was often sent to stay with his grandmother, a full-blooded Cherokee Indian, who lived in Vancouver, Canada. However, his mother died while he was young which provided a slightly more stable home situation, but he had to start work at the age of sixteen to supplement the family income, which suffered from seasonal fluctuations. Even before that, Jimi had become interested in the guitar, apparently miming with a broomstick at the age of ten and his father bought him a guitar at the age of twelve. In those early days, his main musical interest was the blues, with special reference to B.B. King, Robert Johnson and Muddy Water, but he also found Eddie Cochran interesting, a somewhat untypical influence in someone of Hendrix's background. While at school he learned to play the guitar, as well as briefly dabbling in the violin and harmonica. He played in public once or twice during this period, but did little of any

significance musically until 1964, after he had served a spell in the US army as a paratrooper, a period cut short after fourteen months when he injured his back coming to earth after a jump.

When he was discharged from military service, Jimi decided to make a career as a musician, and served a varied apprenticeship playing in soul and blues bands around America, backing up such artists as Sam Cooke, B.B. King, Little Richard, Wilson Pickett, Ike and Tina Turner, Solomon Burke and Jackie Wilson, before moving to New York around 1964. There he continued to pay his dues, backing the Isley Brothers, as well as one of the two most famous acts produced by the twist dance craze, Joey Dee and the Starliters, which must have been an incongruous situation for Hendrix. He also briefly led his own band, Jimmy James and the Blue Flames, a curious mix of the names of two popular British blues bands, Jimmy James and the Vagabonds and Georgie Fame and the Blue Flames, but soon afterwards joined Curtis Knight's band as lead guitarist. This resulted in the eventual release of a series of rather uninspired albums, most of the material on them being unrehearsed jam sessions. After that, Hendrix was out of work for a while, until guitarist/blues singer John Hammond Jr. gave him a job at the Cafe Au GoGo in Greenwich Village. It was there that he was spotted by Chas. Chandler, who had been the bass player with the Animals, and Chandler, recognizing Hendrix's potential, signed him up immediately, and took him to London.

Chandler soon organized Noel Redding on bass and Mitch Mitchell on drums, and with Jimi as singer and lead guitarist, they became the Jimi Hendrix Experience. The buzz that circulated around the fashionable sector of London society was fuelled by the fact that John Lennon, Paul

McCartney and Mick Jagger had seen Hendrix play in New York earlier, and they became his advance publicity machine. When he actually played in London, it became obvious that, if anything, the excitement and brilliance of his playing had been underestimated. It was reported that Britain's two up and coming guitar heroes, Eric Clapton and Pete Townshend, went to every Hendrix gig they could during his first few months in the country, and by the time his first single, *Hey Joe,* was released at the end of 1966, Hendrix had become a cult figure in just a few weeks. When the record entered the charts at the beginning of 1967, it was to be the first of four hit singles he achieved that year. After touring throughout Europe, the influence of Paul McCartney got the Experience booked for the celebrated 1967 Monterey Festival, where America, the country he had left to achieve fame, finally welcomed him back as a star. An album was recorded live at Monterey featuring Hendrix and Otis Redding, another black star who reached the peak of his popularity at Monterey, although the record was not released until several years later.

By now, the first Hendrix album, *Are You Experienced?,* had been released, and while not as instantly accessible as the singles (none of which were originally released on albums) it showed the extraordinary power and ingenuity of Hendrix's playing, which, coupled with a stage act where he played the guitar with his teeth, feigned sexual attacks on his guitar and amplifier, and set his unfortunate Fender Stratocaster on fire, had made him the sensation of 1967. As the hits – *Purple Haze, The Wind Cries Mary* and *Burning Of The Midnight Lamp* – were released in quick succession, the seal was set on Hendrix's acceptability to a superhip audience when he was booked to support the Monkees on a tour of America, but had to be removed from the bill after only a few dates when a number of protesting, puritanical associations, including the Daughters of the American Revolution, created an enormous furore. By the end of 1967, Jimi Hendrix was one of the most famous names in rock music, on a par with Elvis Presley, the Beatles and the Rolling Stones.

The next year, however, while even more successful in terms of record sales and concert appearances, also produced its inevitable problems. Noel Redding left the Experience, and a constant supply of drugs and groupies left Jimi tired and confused. However, this was the year when he released what is generally regarded as his finest album, *Electric Ladyland,* a double album which also featured guest stars like Stevie Winwood, Al Kooper and Jefferson Airplane bassman Jack Casady. Hendrix was becoming a bigger star almost daily, but in inverse proportion to his ability to deal with the problems caused by fame. In 1969 the Experience finally broke up, but Hendrix retained Mitch Mitchell for his stunning performance at the Woodstock Festival, where his amazing mutation of the American national anthem, *The Star Spangled Banner,* which was twisted by feedback and effects to the point of extinction, was chosen as the closing sequence of the film *Woodstock,* and must have etched the name of Hendrix on the minds of those few people remaining in the Western world who still didn't know who he was.

At the start of 1970, an experiment with an all-black band consisting of Hendrix with Billy Cox on bass and Buddy Miles on drums was a dismal failure, and most of that year was spent away from the public eye until his appearance at the last Isle of Wight Festival, an occasion where the array of talent even exceeded that at Woodstock. Unfortunately, Hendrix's set was not well received, perhaps due to the fact that he followed twelve hours of music often similar in quality, if not in style, to his own. Within a month, he was dead, choking on his own vomit while asleep, and the world of music had lost one of the greatest innovators it is ever likely to produce. Hendrix had extended the boundaries of the rock guitar, often playing at a frantic speed and at ferocious volume, treating his instrument as a weapon, and wringing sounds from it which simultaneously excited those who wanted to progress, and disturbed those purists who felt that a guitar was not designed to be used as an instrument of destruction. While there have been players subsequently who have claimed that their playing takes up at the point where Jimi left off, and even one man who claims to be the reincarnation of Hendrix, there will never be another guitarist to make such a deep impression on music in such a comparatively short time. Even though the general feeling was that Hendrix was set on a course of self-destruction, what he achieved will remain as a monument to his ingenuity and incredible vision.

REPRESENTATIVE ALBUMS

Are You Experienced   *(Reprise/Polydor)*

Electric Ladyland   *(Reprise/Polydor)*

Live at Monterey   *(Reprise)*

Smash Hits   *(Reprise/Polydor)*

The late Jimi Hendrix at the 1970 Isle of Wight festival. Within a month this archetypal guitar hero was dead.

STEVE HOWE

Among the record buying public a silent majority
exists which refuses to be swayed by fashion or
critical opinion. It has favourite groups, but
they're not usually the ones who are written about
in glowing terms by trendy journalists, in fact
rather the reverse. In spite of the raw deal handed
out by the press, records made by these groups
continue to sell to an audience who know they'll
get what they want. In this category of groups,
Yes comes high on the list. Steve Howe is their
guitarist, and although by now he must be used to
this peculiar position, he, like the other members
of the group, has seen the other side of the coin.

Steve was born on April 8th, 1947, and became
interested in the guitar before he was a teenager.
His first hero was Chet Atkins, then moving on to
jazz players like Wes Montgomery, Kenny
Burrell, Charlie Christian, and the ubiquitous
Django Reinhardt. However, there wasn't much
demand for jazz guitarists in the mid-sixties when
Steve began to play professionally and his first
group, the In Crowd, was formed to play Chuck
Berry staples, then moving on to soul sounds.
By 1966 the group had changed its name to
Tomorrow, and developed a stage act which was
heavily theatrical, but nevertheless contained
some fine music in similar style to Pink Floyd.

Despite a couple of near miss singles, in
particular *My White Bicycle* and *Revolution*, and an
album in 1968, Tomorrow never quite achieved the
success that was widely predicted for them. Their
producer, Mark Wirtz, was involved in an abortive
project known as *The Teenage Opera*. Keith West,
Tomorrow's vocalist, was featured on the hit
single that resulted, after which Tomorrow folded
up. Steve Howe formed a group called Bodast, but
when that came to nothing he joined Yes.

Yes was formed in 1968 by five previously
unsuccessful musicians, who decided to synthesize
rock with music from a number of other sources
including classical, jazz, and emotive film themes.
Early on they achieve a good deal of critical
recognition, reaching a pinnacle with a song, on
their second LP, by Richie Havens, *No Opportunity
Necessary, No Experience Needed*. It was played by
original guitarist Pete Banks with considerable
doses of the wah wah pedal, but when in mid-1970
Banks left, Steve Howe replaced him and the sound
began to change.

The first Yes record on which Howe appeared
was *The Yes Album* which featured an on-stage
favourite titled *The Clap*, a solo guitar *tour de
force* in extreme contrast to the heavily arranged
music which comprised the rest of the group's
repertoire. As well as demonstrating Steve's
dexterity, it was the perfect way to allow the new
member to become quickly accepted as part of the
group. It's a difficult track to describe but there
are traces of ragtime as well as Howe's jazz-based
background contained in its non-stop action.
Another item where Howe showed his skill was
a very popular stage number, oddly unrecorded,
called *Bass Odyssey*, on which both Howe and
Yes's regular bassist played bass guitar, and
traded licks, producing an astonishing and
unique sound.

Another Howe solo on the subsequent Yes album, *Fragile*, titled *Mood For A Day*, showed definite Spanish leanings, but this album was the first to suffer violent critical abuse while the group continued to be hugely popular with record buyers and concert audiences. This peculiar state of affairs continued during the mid-seventies and Howe didn't record any more solos, preferring to remain an integrated member of the group. Rarely interviewed, his few forays into print generally concerned his incredible collection of guitars, and the experimentation which led him, among other things, to become the first guitarist invited to use the guitar synthesizer invented by Walter Sears, an ex-associate of the great Robert Moog. Sears told *Rolling Stone* that 'Steve Howe is one of the best guitarists around, and musically he can probably get a hell of a lot out of the thing.'

Nevertheless, although Howe's personal acclaim was gradually increasing, the group was beginning to stagnate. Various personnel changes failed to restore the initial spark, and although they maintained great worldwide popularity, Yes were no longer making any progress. This manifested itself in a live triple album, *Yessongs*, on which there were versions of a number of the group's on-stage favourites, including another recording of *Mood For a Day*. However the damning criticism of the music press continued, reaching its nadir at the time of the group's decision, in 1975, each to cut solo albums.

In the event, the break of over a year from group projects resulted in a greatly improved attitude when Yes reformed. Howe's solo album was titled *Beginnings*, and he used a variety of his favourite guitars which were generally unsuitable for work with the group. It was reasonably successful, although it must be said that his attempts at singing were less easy on the ear than his guitar playing. Nevertheless he scored on the American charts and the album provided an excellent escape from the claustrophobic confines of the group.

Upon their reformation in 1977, Yes came up with their most accessible offering for several years, *Going For The One*, which even spawned their first ever hit single, *Wonderous Stories*, featured a couple of tracks co-written by Steve Howe – and heralded an end to the run of critical negativism laid on Yes by the music press.

Steve Howe remains the most straightforward member of the group's front line, to a large extent because of his interest in guitars – his vast collection numbers nearly a hundred models, forty of which are Gibsons, of various types. He also possesses a number of Fenders, both Strats and Teles, as well as a twin-necked steel guitar and several acoustic guitars by Martin, plus a variety of other instruments including Rickenbackers, and models by Gretsch, Framus and Danelectro. There is little doubt that this enthusiasm for the instrument will prevent Steve Howe from becoming stale or losing the urge to improve his playing. Already he is technically one of the best guitarists in the world, and although his first attempt at a partially vocal album was not completely successful, it is likely that his next solo offering will be full of interest, while his recently acquired songwriting experience can only improve the work of Yes.

REPRESENTATIVE ALBUMS

With Yes	The Yes Album	*(Atlantic)*
	Going For The One	*(Atlantic)*
Solo	Beginnings	*(Atlantic)*

Steve Howe of Yes, playing pedal steel guitar.

BRIAN MAY

Brian May is one of the youngest guitarists in this book. As a result, it's difficult to start his section with an amazing story which will immediately grab your interest. The fact that he has a cat and dislikes cold feet aren't terribly revealing, any more than the fact that his favourite authors are Herman Hesse and C. S. Lewis. Being in a group whose appeal is mainly to impressionable sub-teens does have its drawbacks. Despite that, Brian, the lead guitarist of Queen, has transcended fashion and got himself taken seriously as a guitarist by a far wider audience than he might have acquired via a few pop hits.

Brian was born in Feltham, a London suburb close to Heathrow Airport, on July 19th, 1947. His father was and is an electronics engineer for the Ministry of Defence, and from an early age, Brian was also interested in electronic technology. Music was also a favourite hobby, however, and Brian was given his first half-sized acoustic guitar at the age of seven, after which he graduated to piano lessons in Baker Street, London. But this was school time, and everything else had to take a back seat to studies with the result that Brian passed every examination he entered for, and won a place at one of London University's most famous institutions, Imperial College. Even so, he had formed a group at school who were known as 1984, and when he went to university, this was replaced by a trio called Smile, whose drummer was Roger Meddows-Taylor, later the drummer for Queen.

Smile in fact made a single for Mercury Records, but strangely it was only released (and very briefly) in America. Its lack of success probably didn't bring Brian down, as he was still studying very hard at college. When he left, he was

awarded an honours degree in physics and mathematics and was destined for a career as an infra-red astronomer, an obscure but apparently satisfying subject at which Brian excelled, to the point where he was invited while still at college to complete his course at one of Britain's most important astronomical research stations, Jodrell Bank in Cheshire. He turned down that opportunity, feeling that the opportunities to make music were likely to be rather less up there than they were in London.

By this time, during the late 'sixties, May had begun to formulate his style. The teenybop magazines later quoted his favourite music as that played by the Beatles, the Who, Cream and Jimi Hendrix, one of the most straightforward declarations there could be in relation to the four guitarists involved in those groups. The all-time hero, though, was Jimi Hendrix, and one of Brian's pre-Queen groups played a May composition, *The Happy Hendrix Polka*.

While still at school, one of the most interesting events in Brian's life was the decision to build himself a guitar. Fired with enthusiasm for the Beatles, the then fourteen-year-old desperately wanted a good quality electric axe, but his parents felt unable to spend the necessary sum of money on what might turn out to be a passing whim. As an alternative, Brian's father suggested that he should help his son to make one, using the electronic flair they shared. The instrument's body was carved from an antique fire place, and Brian and his father designed a special truss rod to prevent the neck of the guitar becoming distended by the pressure of the tightened strings. Mother of pearl inlays in the fretboard were fashioned from buttons, and other refinements included an adjustable bridge, a

tremolo arm which is claimed to retract more efficiently than any other guitar currently on the market, hand wound pickups which produce a tone that is probably unique, and an ability to accentuate feedback. Quite an achievement for an employee of the Ministry of Defence and a schoolboy, but the guitar, which apparently took two years to complete, cost little more than eight pounds, a distinct saving especially since Brian still uses the instrument today for both recording and live work.

After the demise of Smile, when the group's vocalist/bass player decided to leave, May wasn't sure what to do, and worked ironically enough for the electronics division of EMI, later Queen's recording company in Britain. Then one Freddie Mercury, a friend of the departed Smile member, decided that he wanted to join Brian and Meddows-Taylor, and Queen was conceived during 1973, completed by bass player John Deacon. Before they released their first single and album, it was decided that the group should put out a single under the name of Larry Lurex, the songs being a couple of oldies in *I Can Hear Music* and *Goin' Back*, which had both previously been hits in versions by the Beach Boys and Dusty Springfield respectively. Quite why this decision was made has never been properly explained, but doubtless the decision had something to do with the fact that Gary Glitter was at the height of his popularity in Britain at the time. Nothing happened to the single, which subsequently, of course, became an in-demand collector's item when it was revealed who Larry Lurex and his friends really were, but it was closely followed by Queen's debut single, a Brian May song titled *Keep Yourself Alive*. Immediately, music paper critics latched onto the fact that Brian's guitar work contained echoes of both Hendrix and Townshend. Although neither that single nor the eponymous album from which it was taken made much impact in Britain at the time, the album rose swiftly up the American charts, although it failed to make either *Keep Yourself Alive* or Freddie Mercury's *Liar* into the hit singles they deserved to become.

1974 was the year when Queen really came into their own. The first hit single *(Seven Seas of Rhye)* and another hit album in *Queen II* appeared in the first half of the year, and later on another big single – *Killer Queen* – was taken from another hit LP, *Sheer Heart Attack*. Other outstanding tracks are *The Prophet's Song*, an onstage *tour de force* where he uses the full potential of the special effects built into his home-made guitar to produce a regular show stopper and *Brighton Rock*, where,

by a series of echo effects, he plays in unison with several previously played phrases which are delayed, an experience which cannot adequately be described verbally, but has to be seen and heard to be believed. Queen were definitely on the way to enormous success, and while the group's obvious focal point was Freddie Mercury, who had developed a stage act combining outrageous bisexuality with masterly vocal power, he was often upstaged by Brian May's astonishing guitar work. It's not generally recognized that Brian has contributed some of Queen's best material, including songs like *Now I'm Here* and *Good Company*.

Perhaps his most familiar work is on the gargantuan *Bohemian Rhapsody*, the six-minute-plus single which remained in the British singles chart for four months, and stayed at number one for an astonishing eight weeks. After that, whatever Queen did was going to be an anti-climax, and certainly since the release of that single and its companion album, *A Night At The Opera*, the group have been remarkably quiet, although there have been subsequent records which have failed to make such a vast impact. Despite this lull, Queen remain enormous favourites on stages all around the world, and a large part of their success is due to the chemistry which makes up the group. While Mercury is a perfect front man, May is able to typify the guitar hero, and to have such contrasting personalities who appeal to both female and male audiences (in much the same way that Roger Daltrey and Pete Townshend combine in the Who), is masterly.

It would not be wrong to conjecture about the group's future. While Brian May has come to great prominence in this manner, it seems reasonable to wonder whether his ultimate desire might be to lead a rather less frivolous group of his own, in which he can properly display his fine guitar technique, which, although it is heightened by technological effects, remains an advance on certain areas previously explored by Pete Townshend and especially by Jimi Hendrix. A major part of Brian's potential, of course, continues to rest on the fact that his home-made guitar is capable of sounds others only dream of, but its duties are shared by a Gibson Les Paul.

REPRESENTATIVE ALBUMS

Queen　　(*Elektra/EMI*)

Sheer Heart Attack　　(*Elektra/EMI*)

A Night At The Opera　　(*Elektra/EMI*)

News Of The World　　(*Electra/EMI*)

Brian May in concert at the time of Queen's first major hit record, Bohemian Rhapsody.

STEVE MILLER

'The Grateful Dead and the Jefferson Airplane barely knew how to tune up at that time – and they only knew about four songs. The big highlight was both bands playing *In The Midnight Hour* out of tune for 45 minutes. I knew we couldn't miss. It took me no time to put together a band which could play 25 songs, tight and in tune.' Considering the status of both the bands mentioned towards the end of the 'seventies, it's not difficult to surmise that the quote you just read wasn't referring to recent times. You might also wonder how the speaker had the nerve to criticize such inviolable heroes of the 1967 psychedelic revolution in San Francisco. The answer is that the speaker was Steve Miller.

Not that he was born there – Miller's a Texan, born in Dallas on October 5th, 1943, the son of a doctor. By the extraordinarily early age of five, he was learning how to play the guitar, and before he was a teenager was leading his first group, the Marksmen, who incidentally included another future rock star, William Royce 'Boz' Scaggs. After leaving high school at the start of the 'sixties, the two went to the University of Wisconsin in Madison, and formed another band, the Ardells, who dressed in smart suits and played white soul and rhythm and blues.

During 1965, Miller was attracted to Chicago, the home of the blues music which had become his favourite. There he got to know many famous blues musicians, and jammed with them in the plethora of small clubs which that city supports, later graduating to leading his own band, the World War Three Blues Band. Next, a celebrated keyboard player, Barry Goldberg, who had worked with Paul Butterfield in what was probably the best white blues band of the era, joined with Miller to form the logically titled

Goldberg/Miller Blues Band which attracted record company interest. They signed with Epic Records who were offering more than the ten other companies in pursuit of the band. Unfortunately, a clash of personalities tore the band apart just before they were due to record their first album, and Steve Miller left Chicago, deciding to make tracks towards the West Coast, specifically to San Francisco, where it was rumoured that an exciting musical scene was swiftly developing.

As already indicated, Steve found the level of musical competence wasn't as high as it might have been, so he preferred to send for a couple of friends who were still playing back in Madison rather than trying to form a band from the limited talent pool which existed in San Francisco at the time. By the end of 1966, the Miller Blues Band, later renamed the Steve Miller Band, was a working unit. That first line-up of the band stayed together until the early summer of 1967. Miller and his band made a distinct impression, quickly becoming regulars at local venues like the Matrix, the Avalon Ballroom and the Fillmore Auditorium. As a result of this, they were hired, along with two other unsigned bands from the area, Quicksilver Messenger Service and Mother Earth, to contribute music to the soundtrack of a film called *Revolution*, a semi-documentary which revolved around the generally drug-induced 'happenings' in the area. When a soundtrack album was eventually released, the Miller Band was successfully on record.

Their next recording venture was again not as sole headliners – they were invited to provide the backing for a live album recorded by Chuck Berry at the Fillmore, and while the resulting record could not be termed one of the high points of Steve

49

Miller's career, it nevertheless provided the band with useful experience. Soon afterwards, they finally signed their own recording deal, with Capitol Records, who had been slow to pick up on the San Francisco action, with the result that they were the only major label during autumn 1967 without a San Francisco band on their roster.

After a certain amount of juggling with the personnel of the band, Miller sent for his old friend Boz Scaggs in September 1967, and the latter returned from Europe, only to have to return immediately to London, where the Miller Band decided to make their first album, *Children of the Future*. Miller was able to use material which he had written just after leaving university in Madison, and with the addition of futuristic (for the time) sound effects the album was a great success. Although it has not perhaps worn as well as it might have, it is still regarded by many as a very representative example of progressive rock of the late 'sixties. Still better was the group's second album, *Sailor*, which was also released in 1968, and contains a number of memorable songs like *Dear Mary, Quicksilver Girl, Living In The USA* and *Song For Our Ancestors*. Again using a variety of sound effects, but this time combining them most successfully with his quite excellent original songs, topped off by some staggering guitar playing which displayed a regard for pure pop music and psychedelia as well as the blues, Miller put together an album generally agreed to be among the best two or three to emerge from the first wave of San Franciscan music.

Between the years from the release of *Sailor* until late 1973, Miller continued to increase his following steadily with a series of generally unsensational, but supremely professional albums. Scaggs left after *Sailor* to embark upon what has now become a highly successful solo career and a considerable number of musicians joined and then left the band, most gaining useful kudos from their spell with Miller, but reportedly usually leaving to take up better offers. It was beginning to look as though Steve Miller, long regarded as one of the best musicians to rise out of San Francisco, was destined to be a perennial member of the second division.

During 1973, Steve and his band went into the studio yet again, to record what would be their eighth album in six years. As usual, a track was extracted from it for release as a single, and in this case it was the album's title track *The Joker*, a tongue-in-check potted autobiography of Steve Miller, which referred back to several other songs from previous records in which he had portrayed himself variously as 'The Gangster of Love', 'The Space Cowboy', and a character named 'Maurice'. This slightly odd formula was a huge success and *The Joker* topped the American singles charts during the months at the end of 1973 and the start

of 1974, also dragging its source album to a high chart position. At that point, having received his just rewards, Miller disbanded his group, and took a well earned holiday for over a year, during which time a good deal of his earlier work, only midlly successful when it was originally released, began to achieve the recognition it had probably deserved all along.

It also became clear that Miller was a far more eclectic musician than his records had generally suggested. It was revealed that he was concurrently working on a number of other projects, varying from an album of Christmas carols through a concept concerning the fate of the American Indian to a modern jazz album also featuring the celebrated Adderley Brothers, Julian and Nat. He had also amassed a large number of other recorded tracks, both before and during his 'sabbatical year' with the result that when he finally did emerge with a new album, *Fly Like An Eagle*, which was released in early 1976, it spawned three hit singles in America, one of them also providing Miller with his first British top twenty entry. Not surprisingly, the success of the singles also resulted in some chart action for the album on both sides of the Atlantic, and a three year old compilation of some earlier material also entered the charts.

Many might regard Steve Miller as very restrained, since he refused to capitalize immediately on the success it had taken him so many years to achieve. However, his long-standing belief in his own talent was justified, so that he now rates as one of the top live attractions in the world, and is assured of being close to the charts at all times with any new release. Over the years, and particularly in view of the variety of projects described earlier, Miller has earned the right to be considered a consummate guitarist, especially of the blues and hard rock. Interestingly, the guitar he plays is a hybrid, a Fender Stratocaster with a tremolo arm and a non-standard neck. Even more curiously, it is a left-handed instrument, which Miller, a right-handed player, uses upside down. Further sign of Miller's versatility on the guitar is shown in another favourite axe, a double-necked Gibson with one 12-string and one 6-string neck.

REPRESENTATIVE ALBUMS

Sailor   *(Capitol)*

Number Five   *(Capitol)*

The Joker   *(Capitol)*

Fly Like An Eagle   *(Capitol/Mercury)*

JIMMY PAGE

When Led Zeppelin's *Physical Graffiti* album was released in 1975, it reportedly passed across shop counters at a rate which outstripped the previous fastest seller for Atlantic Records, *Led Zeppelin II*, which shifted a mere 100,000 copies per week. As a group, Led Zeppelin have remained together since their inception at the end of 1968, and they are generally recognized as being one of the top five bands in the world, a position which they have held since they first achieved it within a year of their formation. The idea for the group was conceived by their ace guitarist, Jimmy Page.

James Patrick Page was born in 1944 at Feltham, near London Airport, and during his teenage years was strongly influenced by rockabilly/rock'n'roll guitarists like Scotty Moore (Elvis Presley's original guitarist), James Burton, and 'any of those guitarists who were bending strings – all the earthier ones'. By the time he went to art college, the system which produced so many musicians for the British blues boom, Page had become a promising guitarist and began to play in pickup groups around London, soon gaining a good reputation. He was soon in some demand as a session musician among the newer, up-and-coming groups like the Kinks and the Who, who no doubt felt that he would be more receptive to their requirements than the majority of much older players. During this period Page was rated by many as the number one session guitarist. Of course, apart from this kind of prestigious work, Page also worked on sessions which produced muzak for supermarkets, as well as playing live dates with a diverse selection of people, from Carter-Lewis and the Southerners to beat poet Royston Ellis.

Around this time in the mid-sixties, Jimmy began to experiment with Indian music, and was

the first known British musician to own a sitar. However, he decided probably wisely, to restrict his playing of the instrument to informal occasions, feeling that the instrument would be cheapened if too many people began to use it on record. At the same time he did credit George Harrison with the best recorded work on the instrument. Also during this period (1964–1967), Jimmy began to produce records, probably his best known work of the time being a single released on Immediate Records, *I'm Your Witch Doctor/Telephone Blues*, by John Mayall and Eric Clapton, together with a single by German chanteuse Nico, who was later in the Velvet Underground. A less happy result of the alliance with Immediate was the release of a series of informal jam sessions which featured, among others, Page, Eric Clapton, Jeff Beck, Nicky Hopkins, and several members of the Rolling Stones. The tracks were never designed for release by the musicians involved, but due to their inexperience in business matters, they were persuaded to hand over the tapes to Immediate, and the material – enough to fill two double albums – has been released several times on various labels around the world, including RCA and Sire in the United States.

In July 1966, Jimmy Page joined the Yardbirds, after several years as a session player. He had been invited to join the previous year when Eric Clapton left the group to join John Mayall, but had refused, so Jeff Beck joined the group instead. However, Jimmy was impressed by what the Yardbirds were doing, and would sometimes go with them to gigs, so was on the spot when the group's bass player, Paul Samwell-Smith, decided to leave. Although he claims never to have played bass before, Jimmy took the job, the intention being that eventually he would change places with the group's rhythm guitarist Chris Dreja, who would move to bass and allow Page and Jeff Beck to form a twin lead guitar front line. This remarkable combination unfortunately only continued until the end of 1966, when Jeff Beck left the group. The Yardbirds, with Page as lead guitarist, carried on until July 1968 as a quartet, until singer Keith Relf and drummer Jim McCarty both left to move in new directions. An attempt to form the New Yardbirds was unsuccessful.

At this point Page and his manager Peter Grant auditioned a singer from Birmingham, Robert Plant, who in turn recommended a drummer friend of his, John Bonham. A session playing friend of Page's, John Paul Jones, also asked to join, Keith Moon came up with the name, and Led Zeppelin was born in late 1968.

Since that time, of course, just about everything the group has been involved with has been an unqualified success. In no small measure this has been due to Jimmy Page, who has been the group's producer throughout their career, and has also written a large proportion of their material. Added to that is the wide range of styles he is able to produce from his guitars on the group's records, from the light acoustic feel which begins *Bron-Y-Aur Stomp* on *Led Zeppelin III*, and the unforgettable riff which is the basis for *Whole Lotta Love* on *Led Zeppelin II*, to a variety of astonishing and sometimes extended hard rock solos on various songs on each of the group's albums. Page uses an array of special effects, including the normal fuzz, echo and so on, but also plays his guitar with a violin bow to produce a unique effect, and uses a pedal steel guitar in the studio.

By 1977, each of Led Zeppelin's eight albums had been awarded a platinum disc for sales of over one million copies, and their fourth album had spent over four years in the American album charts. Zeppelin have outlived almost every other group in the world maintaining extraordinary consistency, and have a fanatical following which will guarantee that their carefully planned live appearances, which are comparatively rare to ensure continued sufficient demand are always hugely over-subscribed. The group's music, originally Page's conception, but now very much a trademark of each member of the group, is hard hitting, 'heavy metal' rock for much of the time, but this is leavened with the subtlety of more relaxed material, continually building to natural and vibrant climaxes. That's not to mention the group's visual appeal, which has been described in *The Encyclopedia Of Rock* thus: 'Onstage, they [Page and Plant] are opposites and complements, Plant a golden ringleted Adonis marvellously parodying the sexual superstar while singing in a voice of limitless power, Page a dark fragile guitarist of immense versatility and command clothed in black velvet and rippling dragons'.

Jimmy Page possesses a wide range of instrumentation, but his favourite instruments include a Gibson Les Paul Custom dating from the 'fifties, a Gibson SG with two necks (12-string and 6-string) and a Fender Stratocaster. There is little doubt that he will be among the front rank of rock guitarists until he decides to give up playing – even if that should happen quite soon, he has achieved enough to be remembered as one of the all time greats.

REPRESENTATIVE ALBUMS

Led Zeppelin   *(Atlantic)*

Led Zeppelin II   *(Atlantic)*

Physical Graffiti   *(Swansong)*

KEITH RICHARD

Whenever discussion gets around to favourite bands, or even to the lofty heights of the best band in the world, there's really only one band which will consistently figure in the conversation and that band is the Rolling Stones. They've remained at the top of the most competitive business there is, and as we approach the 1980s, there's no other active band who have been going nearly as long as the Rolling Stones. Consider the others who might be mentioned – there's the Beatles, but they effectively broke up more than a decade ago. The Who – they haven't produced anything worthwhile during the second half of the seventies and Roger Daltrey's career as a film star looks much more likely to continue than his career as a rock singer. The Beach Boys – they're just about together still, but on recent evidence, they're a pale shadow of the group which sang *California Girls* and *Good Vibrations*. The Stones really are the only survivors of the British rock boom of the early 'sixties and their survival has been founded particularly on the relationship between Mick Jagger, a face and name known on Mars, (if there's life on Mars) and his less publicity conscious, but equally important friend and co-writer, Keith Richard. Without one or the other, there wouldn't be a group called the Rolling Stones.

While the group's lyrics are vitally-important, it's the music which frames them that produces the gut reaction and involuntary surge of adrenalin – and that's where Keith Richard comes in, both as writer and performer. Even when Jagger's vocals are an indistinct jumble of shouted words, Keith's guitar keeps up its steady rhythm, controlling the rest of the musicians around him, and ensuring that whatever else happens, the music he wrote will be heard to its best effect.

Keith Richards (his real name has an 's' at the at the end, but he dropped it when the Stones began their career, perhaps to suggest a family tie with Cliff Richard) was born in Dartford, Kent, on December 18th, 1943. His father was an electrical engineer, a profession he hoped Keith would also enter when he started work, but instead of taking after his father, it was his grandfather's footsteps he followed. He had been a saxophone player named Gus Dupree, who had led a dance band before the Second World War, and a country band afterwards. Keith's first guitar, a Rosetti, was acquired during his mid-teens for £10. He soon demonstrated that he was far more interested in the instrument than in his school work, perhaps the first active demonstration he gave of his dislike of authority, which has been a problem for him at various times. He played truant from school, and this led to his expulsion. He was faced with two alternatives – either he would have to get a job, or he could apply to continue his education at the local art college in Sidcup. Not surprisingly, he plumped for the latter course, and at the art college spent most of his time improving his guitar technique in the company of another future rock star in Dick Taylor, an original Rolling Stone, but better known as the leader of the Pretty Things.

Keith's influences at that point, around 1960, were steeped in rock'n'roll, particularly the more uninhibited performers like

Elvis Presley, Little Richard, Jerry Lee Lewis, and his all-time favourite, Chuck Berry. At art school he was also exposed to the quieter and more subtle sounds of folk pioneers like Woody Guthrie and Ramblin' Jack Elliott, which led on to Big Bill Broonzy and Josh White, and thence to Robert Johnson. It was the classic British route to discovery of the blues, one shared by a large number of Richard's contemporaries, and it was on a train journey to London with a Chuck Berry record under his arm that Keith made contact with Mick Jagger. In fact, they had been friendly many years before as children, having lived close to each other, but Keith's family had moved away and the two had lost contact. Having a mutual interest in Berry and the other artists on the Chess record label, like Muddy Waters and Little Walter, the friendship was soon-re-cemented. and together with Dick Taylor, they began to rehearse, although Keith always treated such meetings with more seriousness than the others. who were more intent on conventional careers at that stage.

Various other people drifted in and out of the group – who called themselves Little Boy Blue and the Blue Boys – until 1962, when it was announced in *Melody Maker* that a club was opening in the west London suburb of Ealing, which was devoted to rhythm and blues music, and would feature the only noteworthy British R&B band of the time, Alexis Korner's Blues Incorporated. There the Blue Boys met Brian Jones, who had been doing exactly the same as Mick, Keith and Dick, but in a different part of the country, and Blues Incorporated drummer Charlie Watts. After a period during which all but Keith jammed on stage with Korner's band (he was excluded because his style was too close to Chuck Berry's raunchy rock'n'rolling and too far removed from the blues), they decided to form the Rolling Stones, a group which included Jagger, Richard, Jones, Watts and Taylor, although Taylor was quite soon replaced by Bill Wyman.

Since that time during 1963, the story is familiar – after starving for some months in a condemned house in Chelsea, the group acquired a residency in a pub in Richmond, which was the launching pad for a record contract, supporting appearances on major tours (their first was at the bottom of a bill headed by Bo Diddley and the Everly Brothers) and the first hit singles, *Come On* and *I Wanna Be Your Man*, by the end of 1963. The Stones and the Beatles became the twin spearheads of the first rock'n'roll revolution to stem from Britain, and for several years, Britain ruled the world of pop music.

The achievements of the Stones since those early days are almost too many to be contained in an entire book about them, although numerous attempts have been made – around thirty hit singles, a dozen million selling albums, appearances before enormous crowds all over the world, and a reputation second to none. Of course, there have been as many less pleasant incidents surrounding the group, starting from an early occasion when they relieved themselves on a garage wall in the middle of the night, to the intense displeasure of a petrol pump attendant, and going through numerous more serious brushes with the law, not to mention the death of Brian Jones only weeks after he left the group, and the incident at a free concert at Altamont in 1969, where a member of the audience was killed by Hell's Angels. During the 'seventies Keith Richard particularly has been singled out for attention in the media, not least because of his brushes with the law over alleged drug offences.

Whatever else happens to Keith, and he has experienced many triumphs and as many disasters in a relatively short life, future generations will remember him for both his songwriting talents, which in collaboration with Mick Jagger have resulted in well over half of the Stones' hit singles, and his personification of the rock'n'roll lifestyle. No other musician has so typified the example to be followed slavishly or avoided assiduously – while Jagger has become a jet setting superstar during the 'seventies and no longer represents a threat to parental discipline, Keith Richard has continued to personify the rebelliousness and non-conformity which first attracted fans to the Stones nearly twenty years ago. As one journalist wrote 'When Keith Richard enters a room, rock'n'roll comes in with him', but there's an underlying truth in such overblown statements. During his lengthy career, Keith has collected a large number of guitars, and numbers nearly twenty of them as his favourites, while particularly mentioning a Fender Telecaster and a 5-string custom-made guitar specially built for him by Tony Zemaitis. He will not be forgotten . . .

REPRESENTATIVE ALBUMS

Big Hits – High Tide and
Green Grass   (*London/Decca*)

Big Hits Vol. 2 – Through the Past Darkly
(*London/Decca*)

Rolled Gold   (*London/Decca*)

Made In The Shade   (*Rolling Stones Records*)

Keith Richard has always epitomized the rebel and retains this image after 15 years with the Stones.

CARLOS SANTANA

'I never thought of playing in a band until I was angry enough. I worked in Tic Tocks in San Francisco as a dishwasher – and I got very angry there. I was doing my job so well that they fired the other guy who was working with me, and I had to do the work of two people. Then I thought "Well, if the Grateful Dead can do it – so can I".' Carlos Santana speaking, remembering just how he became a professional musician in 1966, when he was a different dude from today's serene, spiritually aware bandleader whose basic appeal is 'down on the street'. In between then and now Carlos has led nine different versions of his band taking in about forty different musicians, and that has inevitably entailed going through some changes. Oddly, in commercial terms the Santana Band are probably no further forward than when they set out – but they've been through rather more upheavals both personally and musically, than it normally takes to remain stationary.

Carlos Santana was born in Mexico on July 20th, 1947, the son of a mariachi musician, and grew up in Autlan de Novarro. He briefly studied clarinet and violin at school, and turned to guitar in his early teens, although the music he listened to was not what might have been expected. Rather than the heavily rhythmic Latin American music with which he eventually made his name, Carlos was first a fan of blues musicians like B.B. King, Jimmy Reed and Bobby Bland. After an understanding schoolteacher had urged Carlos to choose between his two natural skills, art and music, he began to involve himself wholeheartedly in the guitar, at the same time firing the imagination of his brother Jorge, who later led his own band, Malo. By this time, Carlos had relocated in the United States.

San Francisco was where it all started for

him. After seeing the Grateful Dead leaving their limousine to play in the Fillmore West auditorium and being made to work twice as hard at his menial job, he decided to cash in and form a band, which he called the Santana Blues Band. It included a couple of friends from the Tijuana period, plus keyboard player Gregg Rolie and percussionist Mike Carabello. This lasted for about eight months, until mid-1967, during which time the band did play at the Fillmore West – although Carlos's introduction to Bill Graham, who ran the Fillmore, was less than auspicious since Graham had caught him climbing through a window to avoid paying to see the Butterfield Blues Band. In fact, Carlos himself had already appeared on stage at the Fillmore prior to his own band being booked there, when Mike Bloomfield, guitarist with the Butterfield Band, had invited him to jam after a recommendation from a mutual friend. This might have taken his music in a different direction had not destiny struck up and put Carlos in hospital for three months, during which time his blues band broke up.

Just before that happened, Carlos had been spending a lot of time hanging around an area of San Francisco known as North Beach. As he said, 'I used to drink some wine, smoke some grass, and just listen to the conga players while I watched the sea – seven conga players trying to get it off at the same time'. One of those conga drummers was Marcus Malone, and although he subsequently faded from the picture, he is generally credited with being the first person to interest Carlos in the all-pervading 'Latin' rhythm which has been a feature of his music ever since. Marcus and Carlos, together with Gregg Rolie and bass player David Brown formed the first band to be called Santana, and began to attract a good deal of local attention,

finally coming under the management of Bill Graham, who was (and is) the most influential non-musician in the San Franscisco rock scene. It wasn't long before the group were headlining at the Fillmore, above bands who already had the recording deal which was obviously the next logical move for Santana. Part of the reason for this success, over and above the influence of Marcus Malone, was the fact that Bill Graham had persuaded the band to include in their repertoitre a song written by a famous Latin-American musician, Willie Bobo, called *Evil Ways*, which soon became the high point of their set. In fact, by mid-1969 Malone had left the band, and was replaced by two percussionists. Mike Carabello had returned after being fired from the Blues Band for refusing to rehearse while Carlos was in hospital. The second percussionist was the self-styled Nicaraguan 'superstar' (he professes to be the third most popular person in Nicaragua) Jose 'Chepito' Areas. With this line-up, the group signed with CBS/Columbia Records, and received the perfect opportunity to launch themselves when Bill Graham somehow got them booked to play at the Woodstock Festival. This resulted in vast sales for the group's first three albums, *Santana, Abraxas* and *Santana – The Third Album,* with *Abraxas* eventually selling well over two million copies, and including several songs which continue to be among the most popular in the group's repertoire, like *Samba Pa Ti, Black Magic Woman* and *Oye Como Va*. The titles of the songs make the increasing Latin-American influence clear, an influence which was at its peak while Chepito was in the band.

But it wasn't to last. Just when they seemed to be at the peak of their creative ability, they were beset by numerous problems – Chepito developed a brain tumor (he subsequently recovered and rejoined the band in 1973), and several of the other members of the band were strongly affected by drug indulgences, which together with ego battles and inefficiency all combined to prolong the recording of *The Third Album* over nearly a year. After a South American tour which had previously been arranged, but which was 'a disaster', due to the band's lack of unity, Carlos disappeared for nine months, only once briefly reappearing for a festival held in the crater of a volcano in Hawaii, where he played with Buddy Miles. By September 1972, he resurfaced with an almost completely new line-up, this time combining jazz influences with the Latin music and rock which the band had previously played. The result was a pair of albums which are generally thought of as representing Santana's 'middle' period, *Caravanserai* and

Carlos Santana was one of the first guitarists to blend hot Latin American rhythms with hard rock.

Welcome. Many respected critics feel that this was the most satisfying version of the band, and perhaps the reason for this was that Carlos had been introduced via John McLaughlin to the teachings of the Indian mystic Sri Chinmoy, who cured him of his drug problems.

Despite achieving a measure of stability in his personal life, Santana's band was still subject to constant personnel upheavals. Perhaps to combat these disturbances, he made a devotional LP with fellow disciple McLaughlin titled *Love Devotion Surrender,* which was dedicated to Sri Chinmoy, but several other albums released during this period reflected his lack of direction, being nebulous collaborations with other Chinmoy converts and modern jazz musicians. During mid-1975, however, Bill Graham, who had been manoeuvred away from Santana in 1970, began to manage the band once more, and their fortunes began to change for the better, with a partial reversion to the style of music played on the early albums, although with personnel who were considerably more adaptable. After a highly successful European tour, during which Santana revealed that, rather like McLaughlin, he felt he had learned enough from Sri Chinmoy, and would be following his own spiritual path in future, another vastly different line up recorded *Amigos* which became the first Santana LP to make the American top ten since *The Third Album*. That was in 1976, since when the band have consolidated their position, without really progressing too far – but giving their audience what it wants.

Although Carlos has from time to time been upstaged by the members of his band and other external circumstances, his vision of the fusion of Latin-American music with his own strong blues-rock guitar has singled him out as a unique figure. After a long period using Gibson guitars, Carlos now prefers a custom built guitar made especially for him by Yamaha, but also uses a Gibson Flying V and a Fender Stratocaster. He seems to have acquired a measure of self-confidence during the latter half of this decade, and if his contentment persists, there seems no reason why this man, who has already been a notable innovator, should not take his playing into as yet uncharted directions.

REPRESENTATIVE ALBUMS

Abraxas   *(Columbia/CBS)*

Caravanserai   *(Columbia/CBS)*

Welcome   *(Columbia/CBS)*

Amigos   *(Columbia/CBS)*

PETE TOWNSHEND

During 1976–77, a musical revolution occurred in Britain, which the media dubbed 'punk rock'. It was an expression on the part of a new generation of their disgust with the values of the hippie 'revolution' of the 'sixties, which outside influences, notably Britain's economic decline, had turned into a bad dream. That revolution's voice was its music, and, while the established stars of older generations, including Elvis Presley, Bob Dylan and the Beatles, and even to a lesser extent, the Rolling Stones, were dismissed as being self-satisfied and incapable of producing anything worthwhile, one star of that era has been immune from such criticism, although the other members of his group were predictably less fortunate. That exception was Pete Townshend, of course – from the time his group, the Who, first exploded on the scene in 1964, Pete Townshend has seemed to represent the voice of frustrated youth, the only person who could verbalize the anger and frustration of a generation whose complaints were ignored by their elders. For such an influence to have transcended two generations is almost incredible considering Pete Townshend's unwillingness to act the part of youth leader.

Pete was born on May 19th, 1945, in Chiswick, West London, the son of a musician. His early years passed comparatively quietly, although it is rumoured that at the age of thirteen, he played in a traditional jazz band, which also contained John Entwhistle on trumpet. At that point, Pete was playing banjo, but in the next two years he took up guitar and began to get involved in rock'n'roll, undoubtedly being influenced by Eddie Cochran on the one hand, and the Shadows on the other. In 1960, he joined a local group called the Detours, which was led by Roger Daltrey on lead guitar, and and again included Entwhistle, who by this time

had learned to play bass. Townshend was at art school by this time, and spent his spare moments going to the legendary Ealing Club in West London, where he saw the Rolling Stones, Rod Stewart and many of the other musicians who would later form the backbone of the British R&B/beat group movement of the early 'sixties.

The Detours, with a vocalist named Colin Dawson and drummer Doug Sanden, changed their name to the High Numbers at the instigation of their manager, and acquired a recording contract with Fontana Records, although by the time they went into the studio, Daltrey had moved to vocals instead of Colin Dawson, and Sanden, who was apparently fifteen years older than the rest of the group, had been replaced by Keith Moon. The group's debut single, *I'm The Face/Zoot Suit* was not a great success, although subsequently it has become one of the most in-demand collector's items in the world, and the group made no further records for Fontana, although they had by now established a large following around the Shepherd's Bush area of London. Following a name change to the Who, the group played regularly in a Club known as the Goldhawk, and appealed strongly to a particular section of British youth who were known as modernists or 'mods', recognizable through their short haircuts, their neat but outrageous style of dress (derived from art schools, and typified by brightly coloured clothes made from extraordinary materials, a prime example of which was Townshend's Union Jack jacket), and their experimentation with chemical drugs. This way of life also made great enemies of another movement of the time, the 'rockers', who wore leather clothing and espoused a lifestyle similar to the Hell's Angels, the result being several

pitched battles between mods and rockers during 1964.

The chosen music of the mods was a combination of various types of soul, with an emphasis on the Tamla Motown sound of Marvin Gaye, the Temptations and all the rest, mixed with the more abrasive work of James Brown, and this was the music played by the Who and the other favourite mod group of the time, the Small Faces. However, both Townshend for the Who, and Ronnie Lane and Steve Marriott for the Small Faces, also began to write their own material, in Townshend's case a mixture of soul and the rock music of the 'sixties. By the time they got another recording deal, he was writing much of the Who's material, although their first two albums also reflected those soul sounds, and included material by James Brown, Bo Diddley and Martha and the Vandellas. Apart from their lurid clothes, the Who's other main trademark in those early days was a stage act which ended in total destruction of their equipment, with Moon and Townshend as the main protagonists. The latter had developed a unique style of playing, which was strongly based on rhythm, and which generally relied for guitar breaks on chord sequences rather than individual notes. Perhaps the nearest equivalent was Bo Diddley, but Bo didn't also leap high into the air, pummel his instrument with an arm like a windmill, and end the performance by swinging the guitar around his head before smashing it down on the stage, where most times it would shatter into pieces. Apart from the visual impact of such behaviour, another by-product was a vicious strain of feedback from the tortured instrument, assisted by Townshend's habit of running towards his amplifier and ramming it, bayonet style, with the neck of his guitar. Inevitably, this wholesale destruction of the group's equipment led to financial problems, but it also helped to establish the Who as one of the most famous names in rock music with a string of hit singles like *My Generation, Substitute, I'm A Boy, I Can See For Miles* and *Pinball Wizard* which led on in 1969 with Townshend's celebrated rock opera, *Tommy*, which was subsequently performed by an all-star cast on stage and made into a film directed by Ken Russell, starring Roger Daltrey in the title role.

By the end of the 'sixties the Who were one of the top groups in the world, appearing at Woodstock, Monterey and the Isle of Wight Festivals, and drawing huge audiences to their exciting, although now less destructive, live shows. However, it was a problem for the group,

Pete Townshend is the father of punk. His wild and sometimes destructive stage act has made him the idol of new wave bands.

and especially Townshend, to come up with anything to follow *Tommy*, and for some time from 1970, the 'deaf, dumb and blind kid' of the title became an albatross around the group's neck. The group rarely got together except when they needed to make a record or were on tour, and Townshend, after a series of unpleasant drug experiences, found solace in the teachings of Indian mystic Meher Baba, although, unlike Carlos Santana and John McLaughlin who strongly espoused the teachings of their chosen 'guru' and later almost completely denounced him, Pete has never sought to preach to others on the subject, but remains a disciple.

Instead he has produced two albums external to the Who, a solo album titled *Who Came First* in 1972, and five years later, a collaboration with ex-Small Face and fellow Baba convert Ronnie Lane called *Rough Mix*. He also became involved in production, working with Thunderclap Newman, who had a big hit with *Something In The Air,* and with a promising duo named John Otway and Wild Willie Barrett. This patronizing of promising talent also manifested itself in his invitation to the James Gang to support the Who on tour, which first brought to public attention the talent of Joe Walsh. Inevitably, his lack of output in the late 'seventies has resulted in public attention being focussed elsewhere, but the punk 'new wave' has brought Townshend as a musician back into the public eye. Many punk bands, in particular The Jam, hold Townshend in great esteem, and have reminded the public that in many respects, the punk revolution contains echoes of the Who more than a dozen years later.

Pete Townshend no longer needs to smash guitars on stage, of course – he doesn't have to attract attention that way any more, added to which there can be little doubt that the anger which provoked such destruction has mellowed to a great extent. His favourite instrument is a Gibson Les Paul, and there are many thousands of faithful admirers who will rush to hear the results when he picks it up again, and leaps on stage, one of the few stars of the 'sixties who will certainly be a star of the 1980s as well.

REPRESENTATIVE ALBUMS

With the Who	Tommy *(MCA/Polydor)*
	The Story Of The Who *(MCA/Polydor)*
Solo	Who Came First *(MCA/Polydor)*
With Ronnie Lane	Rough Mix *(MCA/Polydor)*

JOE WALSH

Jimmy Page said 'He has a tremendous feel for the instrument. I've loved his style since the early James Gang'; Eric Clapton said 'He's one of the best guitarists to surface in some time. I don't listen to many records, but I listen to his'; Pete Townshend said, 'Joe Walsh is a fluid and intelligent player. There aren't many like that around'. Quite a remarkable testimony from three of the finest rock guitar players in the world to one of their kind, perhaps even more remarkable when you consider that Joe Walsh didn't even make a record until the other three were seasoned superstars, and almost literally achieved overnight fame.

Joe was born in New York in 1947 and brought up in the neighbouring state of New Jersey, where he taught himself the guitar. In the early 'sixties, Joe joined a local group called the Nomads, who were Beatle imitators, both visually and musically. In fact, they didn't need a guitarist, but a bass player, but Joe was so anxious to join the group that he lied about his experience with the instrument, and fortunately soon fitted in.

At the end of his high school years, parental pressure forced him to give up that group and go to college, and he enrolled at Kent State University in Ohio, later notorious for the riot of 1970 when five students were shot by the National Guard. With the intention of playing a little music, perhaps in his spare time, Joe took his Rickenbacker 12-string along, but found after a particularly short time that he was not cut out for studies, and dropped out of college, although he stayed in the Kent area, joining a bar band called the Measles at the beginning of 1966.

Before Joe was a member, the group were merely one of a number of local bands, but soon afterwards, with Joe playing lead, they became the hottest group in the area. The next three years were spent as local heroes, until the violence and unrest resulted in the group splitting up to go their separate ways. By then, Joe was something of a celebrity, and almost immediately afterwards he was asked to join a group from Cleveland, the James Gang, which is where he first came to national prominence. Soon after Joe arrived, the group were seen by Bill Szymczyk, at the time a talent scout for ABC Records, and by the end of that year, 1969, only six months after he had joined the group, Joe was on record as guitarist/vocalist of the James Gang.

While Joe was in the group, the James Gang made four albums, the best of which are the first two, *Yer Album* and *The James Gang Rides Again*, but a good deal of the credit for their somewhat mercurial rise to fame is due to Pete Townshend who came across the Gang when they were supporting the Who in Pittsburgh. He immediately invited them to tour Europe as support act for his group, only months after *Yer Album* had been released. Things looked very good for the group, and they toured furiously and with great success for a couple of years, until Joe began to find the guitar/bass/drums format of the group too restrictive for the songs he was writing – they could be put on records, but because of the overdubs used, it was impossible to recreate them on stage.

In 1971, Joe moved west to Boulder, Colorado. There he began to put together a solo career, and also acquired a new manager, Irv Azoff, who had previously been his booking agent, and after six months work, the first Joe Walsh solo album was made under the name of *Barnstorm*, his group at the time.

It wasn't until a keyboard player was added to

Barnstorm that the group went on the road, but the rest had given Joe a good deal of energy, to the point where he led Barnstorm around America for a reported 330 dates in a single year, in support of the group's second album, *The Smoker You Drink, The Player You Get*. This album includes the song which has become one of his most requested on-stage numbers, *Rocky Mountain Way*. Despite the undoubted success of the Barnstorm concept, the group split up at the end of 1973, leaving Walsh to work on his next album. Around this time, he had also begun to play sessions for other people's records, including work with Stephen Stills, B. B. King and Rod Stewart. Joe also got into production, working as both musician and producer on Dan Fogelberg's *Souvenirs* LP, but most of 1974 was spent in experimentation towards the *So What* album, which finally emerged in January 1975, to put on public display the fruits of Joe's labours. Most interest was almost inevitably shown in his interpretation of Ravel's *Pavane De La Belle Au Bois Dormant* played by Joe on synthesizers. The rest of the album, which was the first which Joe produced himself, introduced some of his new found friends in Glenn Frey, Don Henley and Randy Meisner of the Eagles.

Once this album was released, Joe put another band together, this time calling it the Joe Walsh Group, and they toured most successfully, culminating in an appearance at the *Midsummer Madness* spectacular at London's Wembley Stadium in June 1975, where they supported Elton John, the Beach Boys and the Eagles on a bill which will never be forgotten by anyone present. By this time, Joe's ties with the Eagles were getting stronger by the day.

It was therefore almost inevitable that Joe was invited to join the Eagles when Bernie Leadon left the group at the end of 1975. Shortly before this, a fourth Walsh LP had been recorded, *You Can't Argue With A Sick Mind* – a live album which included contributions from Don Felder, Glenn Frey and Don Henley of the Eagles. To many, the idea of Joe Walsh as an Eagle didn't ring

Joe Walsh with the Eagles.
Left to right: Randy Meisner
(who's since left the group),
Glenn Frey, Don Felder and
Joe Walsh.

true – Bernie Leadon, whom he replaced, was very much the most country-oriented member of the Eagles, while Joe was, if anything, into hard rock. However, after working for a considerable period in the studio, the Eagles' sixth album, *Hotel California* (the first featuring Joe Walsh) was released and zoomed to the top of the charts, spawning several hit singles including a Joe Walsh composition, *Life in the Fast Lane*. Critics of the new partnership were most effectively silenced.

As well as being one of the finest hard rock guitarists in the world, Joe Walsh also plays keyboards and synthesizers, but perhaps the item which caused most interest (and confusion) on his first tour with the Eagles was the voice box attachment which enables Joe to play notes on his guitar which he can distort via a tube going into his mouth. Even so, Joe's favourite instrument remains the guitar, and his chosen models are the Gibson Les Paul, and the two Fenders.

REPRESENTATIVE ALBUMS

With the James Gang	Yer Album	*(ABC)*
With Barnstorm	The Smoker You Drink, The Player You Get	*(ABC)*
Solo So What	*(ABC)*	
With the Eagles	Hotel California	*(Asylum)*

SPECIALIST

Duane Allman

The world of rock'n'roll has claimed many victims as a result of the pressures which it inflicts upon its performers. For better or worse, many of those who die prematurely are only appreciated properly in the years following their death, and so it was with Duane Allman, who was killed in a motorcycle accident in Macon, Georgia, on October 29th, 1971.

Howard Duane Allman was born in Nashville, Tennessee, on November 20th, 1946, and his brother Gregg, who was strongly involved in a large part of Duane's career, on December 8th, 1947. When the brothers were still quite young, their father died, leaving their mother to support the family. Discovering that better paid work was to be had in the sunshine state of Florida, the Allman family moved to Daytona Beach in 1959, and soon afterwards the brothers became interested in music, although Gregg was the first to actually acquire an instrument. Duane told interviewer Tony Glover 'Gregg got a guitar for Christmas one year, and I got a motorcycle. I tore up the bike, and Gregg learned to play the guitar. I traded the wrecked parts (of the motorcycle) for another guitar, and he taught me'.

The first group the brothers formed was called the Y-Teens, who played at local youth club dances, their repertoire consisting of material by such as Chuck Berry and Hank Ballard and the Midnighters (original recorders of *The Twist*, later a monster hit for Chubby Checker). Some time later, the brothers were exposed to the blues as purveyed on radio and records by such artists as Robert Johnson, Muddy Waters and Little Walter (Jacobs), and as a result formed the first of the several inter-racial groups they would front.

Unfortunately, even a move to Los Angeles didn't help the success of the records they cut as Hourglass, on the Liberty label.

Duane, meanwhile, had been asked to help out on a Wilson Pickett session which was being recorded at Fame Studios, Muscle Shoals, Alabama. The owner of the studio, Rick Hall, was so impressed with Duane's playing that he signed up the guitarist as a regular member of his session team. and it was in Muscle Shoals during the years of 1968 and 1969 that Duane Allman first began to make the records which would eventually assure him of legendary status. In those early session days, the artists whose records Duane was decorating were normally soul-based, and included, apart from Pickett, King Curtis, Boz Scaggs and Arthur Conley.

Duane's fame soon spread, to the point where he became one of the most in-demand session guitarists in America, travelling to New York to guest on records by Aretha Franklin and Delaney and Bonnie, among others. However, he was reportedly not happy playing exclusively in the studio, and on a trip back to Florida, he got involved in a jam session with all those who would later become the first version of the Allman Brothers, with the exception of his brother Gregg. After that loose jam went so well, everyone involved knew a permanent band would have to result. Duane called Gregg and the Allman Brothers Band was formed. They recorded two under-rated albums, which were eventually re-released under the title of *Beginnings,* and when his own band were not playing, Duane was still able to fit in a number of sessions, including his unforgettable duet with Eric Clapton on *Layla*.

During March 1971, the Allman Brothers Band recorded an excellent live double album at New

York's Fillmore East, which finally established them as one of the leading groups in the world. During that same summer, they were putting down tracks for the next LP, which eventually came out as *Eat a Peach*, when Duane had his accident. Despite three hours emergency surgery, he died and the album was completed without him.

Perhaps the best way to describe Duane Allman's guitar style is to quote the words of Jerry Wexler, famous record Producer and Vice-President of Atlantic Records, for whom much of Duane's best work was done: 'He was a complete guitar player, he could give you whatever you needed, he could do everything, Play rhythm, lead, blues, slide, bossa nova with a jazz feeling, beautiful light acoustic – and on slide he got *the* touch. A lot of slide players sound sour – to get clear intonation with the right overtones – that's the mark of genius. Duane is one of the greatest guitar players I ever knew – he was one of the very few who could hold his own with the best of the black blues players.' While Duane Allman used many different types of guitar to achieve the various sounds described by Jerry Wexler, his preferred instruments when playing rock and soul music were the Gibson Les Paul and the Fender Stratocaster and Telecaster.

Representative albums

The Allman Brothers	The Allman Brothers Band at Fillmore East *(Capricorn)*
Duane Allman	An Anthology *(Capricorn)* An Anthology Vol. 2 *(Capricorn)*

Jeff Beck

It's more than a little ironic that all too many people know of Jeff Beck merely because it was in one of his groups that both Rod Stewart and Ron Wood first made any impression on the record buying public. This is also more than a bit unjust, since during the 'sixties, Beck was ranked alongside Eric Clapton and Jimi Hendrix in the roll of honour of British blues guitarists. It has to be said that only his refusal to compromise has prevented Beck from becoming as great a popular hero as he is a critical choice.

Born on June 24, 1944 in Surrey, England, Jeff singing in church choirs and receiving tuition on a variety of instruments, so that by the time he left school and went to Wimbledon Art College, he was an adept blues guitarist.

There was some doubt in Jeff Beck's mind about becoming a full time professional musician, but

that was soon erased when he was asked to replace Eric Clapton in the Yardbirds, to whom he had been recommended by Jimmy Page, yet another star to emerge from the outer London R&B scene. That was in March 1965, and the first Yardbirds record he played on was *Heart Full Of Soul*, which was a big hit, going top ten on both sides of the Atlantic during the second half of 1965. Jeff's work with the Yardbirds was consistently good during the year and a half he stayed with the group, a period which produced the final five hit singles that they scored, most of which can be found on various *Greatest Hits* albums by the group. In fact, during 1966, both Beck and Jimmy Page, who had joined the group initially as bass player, but soon after switched to lead guitar, were playing twin lead, although only two recorded tracks featuring this million dollar duo were released: *Happenings Ten Years Time Ago* and *Psycho Daisies*.

Quite why Beck decided to leave the Yardbirds doesn't seem to have ever been explained properly. For whatever reason, Jeff took a six month break after leaving the group, and claims that he didn't even pick up his Telecaster during that time. After that hiatus he was briefly involved in session work again at the instigation of his old friend Jimmy Page, and during that period changed his guitar for a Gibson Les Paul. During the early part of 1967, starmaker Mickie Most began to take an interest in Beck's career, and signed him up to make solo records, the first of which instantly became a hit in May 1967. The song involved was a peculiarly 1967 artefact, *Hi Ho Silver Lining*, which featured Jeff singing as well as playing guitar, and the B side of the record – *Beck's Bolero* – has become a collector's item, because it is played by a trio of Beck, Page and Keith Moon of the Who.

After that, it was time to get a group together for live performances, and the first Jeff Beck Group was completed by Rod Stewart as singer, Ron Wood on bass, and a succession of drummers. In 1968, the group first toured in America, where they caused a sensation, partially because their debut album, *Truth*, was released and sold over a quarter of a million copies in a very short time. It contained a mixture of the greatly inspired and the average, with particular praise being heaped on *Morning Dew* (a Tim Rose song), Howlin' Wolf's *I Ain't Superstitious*, and strangely enough, a reworking of *Old Man River*. Despite the fact that the album is patchy, many still consider it to be the best work ever done by either Beck or Stewart, before or since.

During the recording of the following album, *Beck Ola*, Ron Wood was fired and things began to go wrong, with the group finally collapsing during 1969. Soon after, Beck had an accident which kept him out of action for some time.

In mid-1972, Carmine Appice and Tim Bogert of

Vanilla Fudge contacted Beck with a view to forming what each considered might be their 'dream group'. When the group made an album, simply titled *Beck, Bogert and Appice*, it was obvious that in terms of their instrumental ability, there were few bands which could touch them, but unfortunately this was not matched by the vocals, and by 1973, yet another Jeff Beck enterprise had crumbled to nothing. For over a year nothing was heard from him. In 1975, he re-emerged using the production talents of Beatles producer George Martin, the result being a totally instrumental album titled *Blow By Blow*, where his leanings towards jazz, previously demonstrated on the post-Rod Stewart, pre-Bogert and Appice albums, were taken a step further. A similarly jazz tinged follow-up, *Wired*, came out in 1976, which also featured appearances by various associates of John McLaughlin, and by 1977, Beck was sharing billing with jazz/rock keyboard player Jan Hammer.

It has often been said that Jeff Beck promised rather more than he usually produced on record, and such a judgement is difficult to deny. From his blues period, through the Yardbirds (the inspiration for numerous late seventies American groups) to the group with Rod Stewart, Beck's output, although inconsistent, could always be relied upon for fireworks. Since that time, his apparent need for experimentation (he even played with Stevie Wonder at one point) has led him further and further away from the hard rock which many consider he does best, and into a rather more nebulous area where any nod towards commerciality seems to have vanished. Interviewed in *Circus* magazine, Beck explained his motivation thus: 'There's no gradual development from the Yardbirds to the albums with Rod to the second Jeff Beck Group to *Beck, Bogert and Appice* to *Blow By Blow* and what I'm doing now. I just stop playing, and when that particular project is over, then millions of miles will go under the bridge. Then I just start playing again and whatever happens, happens.'

Like several of his peers, Jeff Beck has had a number of his guitars stolen over the years, but now uses either a Fender Stratocaster or a Gibson Les Paul Custom. As he says 'If you want to play fat long chords that distort, or a thicker, sort of woodier sound, use a Les Paul. But for really frightening get down rock, the Strat is the guitar – it screams!'

Representative albums

The Yardbirds   Greatest Hits   *(Epic)*

Jeff Beck   Truth   *(Epic/Columbia (UK))*

Beck, Bogert & Appice   *(Epic)*

Ry Cooder

'Ry Cooder is an artist in the true sense of the word – a man who makes his craft a fine art. As such, his actions aren't governed by commercial considerations. He operates very much on the outskirts and often at the frontiers of popular music, rediscovering forgotten musical traditions and reworking lost songs, always adding to them, stamping them with his own distinct style, yet retaining their historical essence.' That was written by Andy Childs in *Zigzag* magazine in late 1976, and seems to encapsulate the reasons why Ryland Cooder has become a cult figure with an ever increasing following.

Jeff Beck

Ry was born in Los Angeles on March 15th, 1947, and was given his first guitar at the alarmingly early age of three. When he was still only ten, his father, detecting a certain promise in his son's playing, bought him a Martin guitar. At thirteen Ry discovered bluegrass via some records he acquired of Appalachian finger picking guitarists, and as soon as he was old enough, spent all his spare time watching the established blues and folk artists who played at the Ash Grove Club, sitting right in the front row so that he could memorize the fingering they used. A particular favourite at this time was the elderly bluesman, Rev. Gary Davis.

At the age of sixteen, Cooder appeared at the Ash Grove as a performer, and by the end of 1963, he had formed an unsuccessful blues duo with Jackie De Shannon, who later achieved her own fame as a singer and writer. This led on to further musical discoveries for Ry, such as the bottleneck style of playing the guitar, and the technique of the banjo. Finally in 1964–5, he found himself in a group with other musicians on his wavelength, including Taj Mahal and drummer Ed Cassidy. The group, the Rising Sons, were signed to Columbia Records, but although they went into the studio to make an album, only a single was ever released.

During the latter part of the 'sixties Ry spent most of his time as a session player, for which he was greatly in demand, playing on records by the Rolling Stones, Paul Revere and the Raiders, and Longbranch Pennywhistle, of which Glenn Frey, later an Eagle, was a member. His connection with the Rolling Stones allegedly could have lasted much longer, but friction developed over whether Cooder or Keith Richard was the originator of the distinctive introductory riff to *Honky Tonk Women*, and little of his work with the Stones was ever released.

He made his debut in 1971 with *Ry Cooder*, an album which created a stir when it was released due to its eclectic choice of material, taking songs from the era of the American depression like Woody Guthrie's *Do Re Mi*, and mixing them with various blues tunes and a much more up to date item by Randy Newman. A similar mixture could be found on his next two albums, but by 1974, when he released *Paradise And Lunch*, the recipe had altered somewhat to include rather more up-tempo songs like *It's All Over Now*.

It was not until his fifth album, *Chicken Skin Music*, that Ry finally procured a wider audience. The album featured music which he had not previously recorded: Hawaiian and Tex-Mex,

Ry Cooder has brought many ethnic influences, especially Mexican and Hawaiian, to enhance his interesting and off-beat music.

the music of the Rio Grande between Texas and Mexico. Interestingly enough, the same Tex-Mex label was given to Buddy Holly's music twenty years earlier, but the music Ry played was of German extraction and featured the accordion. In order to play these new types of music authentically, Ry used both Hawaiian and Mexican musicians, and followed the release of the record with a tour on which his backing group consisted of the Mexicans who had played in the studio. It was this tour which finally began to establish Ry as more than a minor cult figure.

Ry Cooder is a straight speaking idealist, who has given his life to music of various types which interest him. Whenever he comes across a new form which excites him, he will spend sometimes months learning how to master it, and will never record until he feels absolutely ready. Such single mindedness can only be applauded – his desire to play music correctly transcends everything else. His chosen guitars are a Fender Stratocaster for electric work, and a Martin for acoustic playing, although he also uses a variety of other stringed instruments both on stage and in the studio, including banjo, mandolin and an array of exotic instruments indigenous to the areas from which he draws his material. Ry's ability to learn new instruments is almost legendary but perhaps a greater quality is his honesty. It's a commodity that's found all too rarely in all walks of life, but in the music business, it's close to a miracle.

Representative albums

Ry Cooder   *(Reprise)*

Into The Purple Valley   *(Reprise)*

Chicken Skin Music   *(Reprise)*

Jerry Garcia

To a lot of people who listened to rock in the late 'sixties, the greatest music there will ever be came out of the psychedelic movement centred around San Francisco, and the greatest group to emerge from that scene was the Grateful Dead, whose guitarist and generally accepted leader was, and is, Jerry Garcia. The most obvious reason for the longevity of the Dead's – and Garcia's – appeal is the fact that during the 'sixties the group provided a soundtrack for the drug experiments of a generation.

Jerry Garcia was born on August 1st, 1942, in San Francisco, and acquired his first guitar at the age of fifteen, perhaps an advanced age considering that his father had also been a musician. Jerry's initial influence was Chuck Berry, and he taught himself to play the guitar by studiously copying Berry's licks. By this time folk music has begun to make huge strides in California, so Garcia began to study the country music roots of the folk movement, at the same time playing in coffee houses.

Soon his fame on the coffee house circuit was bringing in larger audiences, among whom were Bob Weir and Ron 'Pigpen' McKernan, both future members of the Grateful Dead. In 1962, Garcia purchased a banjo from another future member of the Dead, Bill Kreutzman, and from these brief acquaintanceships came a short lived group known as the Zodiacs, whose members included McKernan, Kreutzman and occasionally Garcia, who would join in on bass when he wasn't gigging as a country/bluegrass guitarist. During 1962–3, Garcia began to organize bluegrass groups with a friend named Robert Hunter, who was later lyricist for the Dead.

After a number of different names the group hit on Mother McCree's Uptown Jug Champions. Unfortunately, by this time jug band music had gone right out of fashion, to the point where the Champions were unable to find enough work to subsist. They were about to split up when

Jerry Garcia of the Grateful Dead, leading lights of 'acid rock', began his career as a folk singer playing in coffee houses, and augmented his income mending broken guitars.

McKernan, whose father was one of the first rhythm and blues disc jockeys, suggested that the group change their repertoire to include electric blues, and their name to the more appropriate Warlocks. By 1965 the group began to change their musical ideas drastically, influenced by the effects of experimentation with the hallucinogenic drug LSD or 'acid' as it became known. At this point, the Warlocks decided that they were no longer a straightforward rock band, but a psychedelic group, and the name of Grateful Dead was adopted at the end of 1965. The group continued to experiment with various drugs while playing until October 1966, when the drug laws were tightened up in California.

Their first album, released by Warner Bros. in 1967, is not a record that makes for easy listening in the 'seventies, mostly due to the group's lack of experience in the recording studio, but the one member of the group who shines through is Garcia, whose guitar work is exemplary. From that point on, Garcia was recognized as the leader of the Grateful Dead, a position which he has maintained ever since. Nevertheless, he could hardly claim to be other than a cult figure, for it seems that opinions are normally polarized about Grateful Dead music – its sometimes meandering qualities are either loved or hated, and Garcia, who can play solos of both blistering directness and annoying pointlessness, is the main cause of that polarization. Of the Grateful Dead's more than a dozen albums released since 1967, the most

popular seem to be *Live Dead*, a 1970 double album recorded in concert, and the succeeding two studio albums, *Working Man's Dead* and *American Beauty*. Jerry Garcia has also made two doubtful solo albums, *Garcia* and *Reflections*.

Whatever is said of Jerry Garcia's guitar playing it cannot be denied that when he is on form he is one of the most fluid and inventive players in the world, capable of transporting the listener for long periods, as can be heard on *Dark Star* from the *Live Dead* album. It's also obvious that the man is held in high esteem by his fellow musicians, as his list of session credits reads somewhat like a 'Who's who' of the Los Angeles scene. He has taken his Travis Bean guitar with its aluminium neck to help the Jefferson Airplane and many of their offshoots; the New Riders Of The Purple Sage, for whom Jerry played as a fulltime member on pedal steel during a period of Dead inactivity; Crosby, Stills, Nash and Young, both individually and collectively; Brewer and Shipley; and It's A Beautiful Day. It may be a cliche, but it applies to Garcia: you either like him or you hate him, but you certainly can't ignore him.

Representative albums

Live Dead   *(Warner Brothers)*

Working Man's Dead   *(Warner Brothers)*

American Beauty   *(Warner Brothers)*

Lowell George

'Credentials? Picture this: Mick Jagger ordered every album from Warner Brothers that the band ever did on his arrival in the U.S. several years ago. Upon hearing their first single, a Rolling Stone writer labelled it "a masterpiece . . . the best record I've heard in months". Seatrain covered one of their songs, and it turned into their most played out of all, and the song has become an anthem of road truckin' ever since. The Byrds did one of their classics and so has Bonnie Raitt.' To read a quote like that in a magazine might give the impression that the band to which it referred must be a thriving and well known institution. Yet Lowell George, the recognized leader and founder member of Little Feat, could say during 1975, 'It was a great hobby, but we weren't making any money. We really weren't surviving'.

Lowell George was born in Hollywood, California, in 1945, and he is probably the only rock'n'roll star to have graduated from Hollywood High School. He was attracted by music at an early age, listening to a wide variety of different types from the modern jazz of Ornette Coleman, through the diverse rhythm and blues produced by Howlin' Wolf on the one hand and Mose Allison on the other, to the rock'n'roll of Chuck Berry and

Lowell George, leader of the hard rock band Little Feat and ex-Mother of Invention.

Little Richard, and even on to the bluegrass of the
Kentucky Colonels. Even so, he didn't start
playing the guitar until the age of 18.

His first pseudo-serious group was the Factory,
who achieved no more than support status.
Next, Lowell became singer of the Standells, a
Hollywood group accepted as being among the
first 'punks'. He then joined Factory drummer
Richie Hayward in the Fraternity of Man.

While he had been playing with relatively
normal groups thus far, Lowell then joined the
Mothers of Invention, led by Frank Zappa, in 1970,
where he was again employed as a singer rather
than as a guitarist. His time with the Mothers has
been confused by the passing of the years, but he
is alleged to have appeared on *Weasels Ripped My
Flesh*, and during 1970, he and bass player Roy
Estrada left the group. Shortly before, George had
cut a demo of a song he had written called *Willin'*,
perhaps one of the ultimate truck driving songs.
Warner Brothers were so impressed with the song
that they allowed Lowell and Estrada to put
together a band, which was completed by Richie
Hayward and and another ex-member of the
Fraternity of Man, keyboard player Bill Payne.
All the group were short of was a name, which was
supplied by Mothers of Invention drummer Jimmy
Carl Black, who had commented on the
diminutive size of Lowell's feet. The group became
Little Feat, and recorded their first album to 1971.
It was an extraordinary record, almost
completely the inspiration of Lowell, embodying
his various influences, to which were added Indian
music, which he had studied for a year, plus
traces of Mexican and Bulgarian folk forms.

The album was a critical success, but a
commercial disaster, a fate which also befell their
next two attempts, *Sailin' Shoes* and *Dixie
Chicken*, which were recorded after Estrada had
left the group. By 1970, Little Feat were at the
point of breaking up when they were offered cheap
studio time. They were able to record *Feats Don't
Fail Me Now*, which achieved a minor commercial
breakthrough and gave them renewed heart,
a feeling reinforced by a highly successful
European tour in early 1975. Since then, the band
have made two more albums, but the over-riding
impression is that Lowell George has grown away
from the band in that time.

Lowell George is established as a hero among
discerning followers of rock music's continuing
progression during the 'seventies both for the
quality of his fine songs, and the always original,
although uncategorizable, lines he plays on his
Fender Stratocaster. His playing still has traces
of the blues, and once when asked what was the
root of Little Feat's music, he said 'It's the same
as the Rolling Stones music, based on Howlin'
Wolf's rhythm section'. Like several other players
in this book, Lowell has extended the boundaries

of rock'n'roll to include types of music which have never previously been eligible, and whatever he does following what seems to be his almost inevitable departure from Little Feat, his fans can rest assured that he won't be standing still.

Representative albums

With Little Feat Little Feat   *(Warner Brothers)*

Sailin' Shoes   *(Warner Brothers)*

Dixie Chicken *(Warner Brothers)*

Nils Lofgren's talent and self-confidence have brought him incredibly quickly to the top.

Nils Lofgren

'I had never even heard of Chuck Berry or Elvis Presley until the Beatles. The Beatles were the first rock'n'roll band I ever heard in my life. I had no concept of AM radio. I just wasn't aware of any music other than classical, so when the Beatles came out, my commitment was total and really intense to rock. I loved it.' Hardly a typical exposure to rock'n'roll for a guitar hero, but then there aren't too many guitar players who are equally at home with an accordian, or who use a trampoline on stage. One who is and does is Nils Lofgren, who spent several frustrating years

struggling for recognition until the world caught up with him, and transformed a dedicated nucleus of followers into a small army. In fact much of his career has been about arriving before he was expected.

Nils was born in Chicago in 1952, and is of Swedish and Italian extraction. From the age of five he was interested in music, but mainly of classical styles, although he did become a skilled accordion player. Then at the age of fifteen he heard the Beatles for the first time, and determined that rock music was preferable. By this time, he lived in Washington, D.C. and played in several high school bands, concentrating on songs from the repertoire of the Beatles, Rolling Stones, Kinks and other British groups. Nils also became aware of Jimi Hendrix.

At the age of seventeen, Nils decided that he's had enough of school, and briefly ran away to New York, where he lived in Greenwich Village. On his return, his parents, seeing that little would be gained by sending their son back to school, encouraged him to form a band, the result being Grin, a trio which featured Nils on guitar, keyboards and vocals with a rhythm section. Most of the group's material was also written by Nils, who was undoubtedly a self-confident youth, as he demonstrated by going into Neil Young's dressing room after Young had played at a Club in Washington, and introducing himself. The evening ended with an incredulous Young listening to Lofgren playing the songs which would be on the first Grin album, and resulted in Young's producer, David Briggs, signing Lofgren to his own record label, Spindizzy, and producing all his records until 1975. More to the point, Neil Young was so impressed with Lofgren's musical ability that he invited Nils to play keyboards on his own album *After The Goldrush*, which many still feel contains the best work Young has ever done. In fact, Nils got on so well with Young and his group of the time, Crazy Horse, that he was invited to join them but although he played on their first album, Nils was determined that if he was going to make it, it would be as leader of his own band.

Grin made four albums between 1971 and 1973, each of them being partially successful, and demonstrating Lofgren's devotion both to Hendrix and a latter day idol, Keith Richard of the Rolling Stones. However, none of the Grin records sold sufficiently to establish the group as anything other than a support act on major tours, and finally Nils broke it up in 1974. It may be that his dramatic arrival on the scene via Neil Young's patronage made it difficult for the public in general to appreciate his precocious talents, but after the break up of Grin Lofgren returned to play with Young on the tour surrounding the latter's *Tonight's The Night* album, and after recharging his creative batteries, came back very strongly with a debut solo record on which he was backed by studio musicians Aynsley Dunbar on drums and Wornell Jones on bass. This was his first breakthrough in commercial terms, and his subsequent albums have reinforced that initial success to the point where by 1977, he had become one of the biggest live acts in the world. To some extent this was due to his stage act, which, apart from the normal paraphernalia of instruments, (his chosen electric guitar is a custom made Fender Telecaster, by the way), boasts a display of acrobatics, in which Nils, while still playing his guitar, performs on a trampoline.

Inevitably, this has led to certain criticisms, with suggestions that Lofgren's talent might be better employed in vaudeville, but there's no doubt at all that he has successfully transcended the change from unsuccessful group leader to a solo star known and respected around the world.

Representative albums

With Crazy Horse   Crazy Horse   *(Reprise)*

With Grin   1+1   *(Spindizzy/CBS)*

Solo   Nils Lofgren   *(A & M)*
       I Came To Dance   *(A & M)*

John McLaughlin

Miles Davis, perhaps one of the most famous jazzmen of all time, and a man continually extending the boundaries of music, is admired as one of the greater innovators, but even he was once moved to remark 'John McLaughlin – he's the one that's the killer. You might hear anything . . .' Certainly, there can be very few musicians who have changed direction with such rapidity and success, but along with that goes the risk that one's audience may not have the ability to keep up.

McLaughlin was born in 1942 in Yorkshire, an unlikely place to produce such an exotic instrumentalist. His mother was a violinist, and that was the first introduction to music for her son, followed by classical piano lessons when he was nine years old, and guitar at eleven. Somehow John got to hear some of the elder statesmen of the blues, men like Muddy Waters, and involved himself in learning to play his instrument in the same way. He also first heard Miles Davis during the mid-fifties – something which was to have a profound effect on his music. As John said, 'He completely rewrote my conceptions of popular music.' By the age of fifteen, McLaughlin's influences included Muddy Waters and Big Bill Broonzy in the blues vein, Miles, Barney Kessel and John Coltrane in jazz, and a smattering of the uncategorizable Django Reinhardt.

During the early 'sixties, he played with a number of seminal British bands who were generally jazz orientated, but also played R&B. Among those bands were Herbie Goins and the Night Timers, Georgie Fame (with whom he recorded the 1964 British number one hit *Yeh Yeh*), and Brian Auger, culminating in a stint with the legendary Graham Bond Organization, which also included Jack Bruce and Ginger Baker, two thirds of Cream. While he was recognized as a fine guitarist, McLaughlin was reportedly awkward and difficult to work with, and it wasn't until 1969 that he was able to make a statement of his own on record, perhaps the reason for his discontent.

That first album, *Extrapolation,* could hardly be termed a commercial success, but it ably demonstrated McLaughlin's command of his instrument in a variety of fields, stretching through jazz, R&B, and also taking in Eastern music. It also reached the ears of Miles Davis through Davis' bass player, Dave Holland. During that same year, McLaughlin emigrated to New York, where he played with Miles Davis, participating in two of the latter's most celebrated albums, *Bitches' Brew* and *In A Silent Way*. During the same period, he also played in another highly rated jazz/rock group, the Tony Williams Lifetime, with whom he also made two albums. The music being made by these groups wasn't to everyone's liking (as Ian MacDonald put it in *New Musical Express* one of the Lifetime albums 'dismayed jazz critics with its wildly distorted electronic sound and rock rhythms, while scaring away rock fans by its bizarre and berserk intensity'). Nevertheless, McLaughlin was now well established as perhaps the foremost jazz/rock guitarist. Despite the critical, if not commercial, success of these various albums, McLaughlin was determined to move on, perhaps even more than before, because of his discovery of and involvement with the mystical religious movement centred around a Bengali named Sri Chinmoy.

The first McLaughlin album dedicated to this new belief was *Devotion*, recorded in France for the small Douglas label, but later purchased and re-released by CBS. This was followed by the solo album *My Goal's Beyond*, featuring the artist playing an Ovation acoustic guitar, sometimes solo, and sometimes with a group, improvising around Indian scales, and it was this album which first introduced the nucleus of the group which heralded what would be recognized as McLaughlin's finest hour, the Mahavishnu Orchestra. This band was formed in mid-1972 and stayed together for over eighteen months, converting a large number of rock enthusiasts to

their music, and making three highly successful albums, *The Inner Mounting Flame, Birds of Fire* and the live album *Between Nothingness And Eternity*.

During this period, McLaughlin also collaborated with Carlos Santana, another Chinmoy convert, to make an album titled *Love Devotion Surrender,* but this project was strangely regarded with rather less favour than the Mahavishnu albums, despite its obvious star content. With the Orchestra, McLaughlin had developed a speed and intensity in his playing which remains unequalled, but despite achieving considerably wider fame than he had previously enjoyed, he still wanted to press further on. He disbanded the first version of the group in January 1974, shortly afterwards assembling a second edition but with somewhat different instrumentation.

During early 1976, it became known that McLaughlin was no longer living the extremely austere life which had begun when he first became a follower of his guru, Sri Chinmoy. He also decided that the Mahavishnu Orchestra had outlived its usefulness. As a result, he formed a group with three Indian musicians which he called Shakti, a name which means 'Creative Intelligence, Beauty and Power', and reverted to acoustic guitar, although by no means a standard instrument.

John McLaughlin's favourite guitar, shown here, is a custom-made Gibson acoustic, with a set of seven 'sympathetic' strings set at an angle to catch the vibrations from the six conventional strings.

It's a Gibson, certainly, but a custom-made model which has six conventional strings plus a set of seven 'sympathetic' vibrating strings set at an angle to the normal six.

It's undoubtedly an exotic instrument, but John McLaughlin has experimented with exotic and often rather disturbing music for most of the latter part of his career. It would not be an exaggeration to say that he has been one of the great innovators on the instrument, although it's open to question whether his work has widened its scope or whether he is now adding a destructive element to his brilliant use of the guitar.

Representative albums

Extrapolation   *(Polydor)*

My Goal's Beyond   *(CBS)*

The Inner Mounting Flame   *(CBS)*

Birds Of Fire   *(CBS)*

Ted Nugent

Ted Nugent is without much doubt the most extreme guitarist the world has ever seen. While residents of New York were complaining about the potential noise pollution of Concorde, Nugent was the subject of complaints after a concert in Kansas City from people who lived as much as fifteen miles from the auditorium, which surely must put him in terms of volume at least equal with a medium sized bomb.

Ted Nugent was born in Detroit, Michigan, in 1949, and took formal guitar lessons from a local teacher for around eighteen months starting at the age of nine. By the time he was eleven, he had organized his first group, the Royal High Boys, and by fourteen was the leader and youngest member of the Lourds, a group whose repertoire revolved around the more raucous items by the Beatles, nearly everything that the Rolling Stones had done up to that point, and a certain amount of Tamla Motown and R&B. Unlike most bands led by fourteen year olds, the Lourds were taken very seriously locally.

In 1964, Ted's family moved to Chicago, although Ted tried unsuccessfully to sabotage the move by destroying several of the removal company's vans. In Chicago, he formed a group, calling it the Amboy Dukes after the name of a then defunct Detroit bar band. He described the way he wanted the band to play by continually making them listen to the first three albums by the Rolling Stones, and this uncompromising stance meant that musicians were continually joining and leaving the band, a state of affairs which actually continued until as late as the mid-seventies. Ted has also been known to admit that his other heroes include Elvis Presley and James Brown (two supreme showmen), Mitch Ryder and the Detroit Wheels, (perhaps the best band to emerge from Detroit in the mid-sixties), Chuck Berry and the Yardbirds.

The Amboy Dukes played around Chicago until their leader was able to leave school, when he thankfully returned to Detroit. As he said '...that was where it was at – the music was always energetic, and everybody was as raucous as hell.' Even so, when the Dukes got there, they soon became the top band in the area because of their greater volume, and in particular Ted's astonishing stage behaviour, which included jumping on top of any piece of equipment he could find on stage, kicking over amplifiers, and even on one occasion biting his drummer's ear until he drew blood. The Dukes were soon in demand by record companies, and in 1967 signed with the predominantly jazz-oriented Mainstream label, for whom they made a first album, *The Amboy Dukes*, in just one day. It showed where Ted's influences lay, with covers of Cream's

I Feel Free, the Who's *It's Not True*, and best of all an extended version of *Baby Please Don't Go*. Before long, Ted, at the age of twenty, decided that he should manage the band as well as lead it. After another album for Mainstream, *Migration*, in early 1969, he left the label.

Still restless and frustrated, Ted fired most of the rest of that group in 1969, and moved to Long Island, New York, where he signed a new record deal with Polydor, releasing *Marriage On The Rocks* in 1969 and *Survival Of The Fittest*, perhaps the best album he had been involved in up to that point, in early 1971. It was a live album, and after its completion, Ted fired most of his band again. He decided that Polydor were no better than Mainstream in terms of record distribution, blaming them for the group's lack of sales in spite of their enormous success on the road.

By 1973, he had formed yet another Amboy Dukes line-up, which made two albums for Frank Zappa's Discreet label, and titled *Call Of The Wild* and *Tooth, Fang And Claw*. (The titles indicated Ted's newest preoccupation – between record deals he decided to hunt for his own meat, which he continues to do, sometimes with guns, but more often with a bow and arrow.) However, Discreet didn't meet with Ted's requirements any more than their predecessors, and it wasn't until he signed with Epic Records in late 1975, this time under his own name rather than as the Amboy Dukes, that he finally felt his record company was behind him.

Ted Nugent is undeniably one of the great characters of rock'n'roll. While what he does on his instrument could hardly be described as subtle in view of the volume he uses, there can be no doubt that Nugent is one of the very best hard rock guitarists in the world, although his use of gimmickry, such as feedback sustained for more than a minute until light bulbs begin to break in the auditorium where he's playing, has an undeniable tendency to detract from his artistry with one of his nineteen Gibson Birdland guitars.

He's also a self publicist second to none, as evidenced by his claim to *Sounds* magazine: 'I've played things live that were just disgusting, and I've played things live that were just the ultimate. I'm sure if there had been any blind people in the audience those times, they would have walked away from the gig able to see'. But perhaps not to hear . . .

Representative albums

With Amboy Dukes	Journeys and Migration *(Mainstream/Pye)*
	Survival of the Fittest *(Polydor)*
	Tooth, Fang and Claw *(Discreet)*
Ted Nugent	Cat Scratch Fever *(Epic)*

Mick Taylor

Mick Taylor's invitation to join the Rolling Stones in 1969 has to be one of the all time good news/bad news stories. It's one thing to be asked to join one of the two most famous groups in the world, but very definitely much less of a good thing when your predecessor, an enormously popular figure, is dead less than a month later. That Mick Taylor survived says a good deal for his self assurance at the comparatively young age of twenty-one.

Mick was born on January 17th, 1948, in Welwyn Garden City, just north of London, and his father worked in the aircraft industry in that area. By the age of 15, Mick had taught himself how to play the guitar. May 1967 saw the formation of Fleetwood Mac by Peter Green. Prior to starting this new group, Green had played for nearly a year in John Mayall's Bluesbreakers, in which he had replaced Eric Clapton. During the time that Clapton had been with Mayall, Mick Taylor had deputised for him on one occasion. As a result, when Green left John Mayall, the latter remembered the seventeen year old prodigy who had been able to fill Clapton's shoes at least adequately, and contacted Mick to take Green's place in the Bluesbreakers. This must have been an opportunity which was just as thrilling for Taylor as his later invitation to join the Stones, and he grabbed it with both hands, playing on some of Mayall's most impressive and enduring albums including *Crusade*, *Diary of a Band Volumes 1 & 2*, *Bare Wires* and *Blues from Laurel Canyon*.

Apart from the chance to play with Mayall,

Mick Taylor replaced Brian Jones in the Rolling Stones line-up in 1969, but left in 1974 to form his own band.

who was recognized as the 'Father of the British Blues', Taylor, like most other up and coming players, was besotted by the blues, particularly as played by Freddie King. However, he was nothing if not ambitious, and by the time he decided to leave Mayall during the first quarter of 1969, was already expressing his desire to play in a wider style than Mayall wanted. He told *Melody Maker* 'I'm not strictly a blues player – I like playing all sorts of things', and had in fact left the Mayall band before the offer came from Mick Jagger to join the Stones. He had no real idea what he wanted to do next until he was invited to the recording sessions for the *Let It Bleed* album, on which he features on *Country Honk* and *Live With Me*. At the time of his joining, Jimmy Page said of Taylor, 'He's an extremely fortunate man, kind of fellow who wins the sweepstakes. All of a sudden he's worth a million dollars – no, maybe more. But he's a nice fellow.'

With the Stones, Mick Taylor played on five albums after *Let It Bleed*, the best of which is probably *Sticky Fingers*, although both *Exile On Main Street* and *Goat's Head Soup* also have their advocates. Due to the group's frequent periods of inactivity, and perhaps coupled with the fact that he was unable to get the Stones to record his own

songs, (although he denied it at the time), Taylor became frustrated with his enforced idleness, and during December 1974 announced that he was leaving the group. Mick Jagger's press release statement said 'After five and a half years Mick wants a change of scene – wants the opportunity to try out new ventures, new endeavours'. These 'new endeavours' in immediate terms meant joining forces with Jack Bruce, who had been the vocalist/bass player of Cream, and had formed a group which also included Carla Bley, who had made her name previously playing keyboards in avant garde jazz circles. As he left the Stones, Mick had said 'I felt I couldn't go much further without some different musicians, so when this chance came to join Jack, I jumped at it, and we've found we have a total empathy. Jack is convinced that the new group will be the best ever – everything is right'. Unfortunately, within six months the band had broken up with both Taylor. But in June 1976, he announced that he had finally formed his own band with several musicians with whom he had worked on the British blues circuit during his time with John Mayall, and during 1977 was signed by CBS Records. He has appeared very infrequently indeed on record since leaving the Stones, and then only on sessions, including work with John Phillips and Elliot Murphy, and had not released anything by his new band nearly a year and a half after they were formed.

Mick Taylor's name is known to almost

everyone interested in rock'n'roll music, but to describe his technique with his Fender Stratocaster or 1954 Telecaster is a problem. While with Mayall, he was a worthy successor to Clapton and Green, moving the Bluesbreakers further into rock and away from the blues, but his role in the Rolling Stones was a little more difficult to define. While Brian Jones whom he replaced, was a player of fills rather than a lead guitarist in the strict sense, Taylor was able to add another dimension to the group, developing a partnership with Keith Richard which the group have never successfully recreated.

Representative albums

With John Mayall   Diary of a Band Vols. 1 & 2 *(London/Decca)*

Bare Wires   *(London/Decca)*

With the Rolling Stones   Sticky Fingers *(Rolling Stone Records)*

Goat's Head Soup *(Rolling Stone Records)*

Johnny Winter

An issue of *Rolling Stone* magazine published the following report from a correspondent in Texas in their issue dated December 2nd, 1968: 'The hottest item outside of Janis Joplin, though, still remains in Texas. If you can imagine a hundred and thirty pound cross-eyed albino with long fleecy hair playing some of the gutsiest fluid blues guitar you have ever heard, then enter Johnny Winter'. It was to be the start of the press coverage of Johnny Winter's career, which has almost always managed to concentrate to a far greater extent on his physical attributes and other sensational items rather than on what is the genuinely remarkable thing about him – his brilliant blues guitar playing.

He was born in Beaumont, Texas, on February 23rd, 1944, the son of a successful contractor who was very keen on music as a spare time activity. In fact, Johnny's father played saxophone and banjo, as well as appearing publicly as a member of a barber shop quartet, while his mother could play the piano. At that rate it wasn't too surprising that Johnny claimed 'I've been playing something ever since I could talk'.

There was also another son in the Winter family, Johnny's brother Edgar, who was three years younger, but equally precocious musically. He and Johnny used to enter (and win) local talent contests playing their ukeleles, and by the time

Johnny reached fifteen years old, he was leading his own band, Johnny and the Jammers. As well as hearing rock'n'roll artists like Chuck Berry, Carl Perkins and Elvis Presley, Winter began to learn about the existence of the blues, which was not a musical form you were very likely to hear frequently in Texas during the late 'fifties. When he eventually did hear the original blues performers, he became fascinated with the music they made, and in 1962 made a 'pilgrimage' to Chicago where he had a friend who owned a record shop. When the friend let him play his guitar in the shop, Johnny was soon festooned with offers of work as a result of which he got to know several of the white blues players who were by then beginning to recognize the incredible blues heritage of America, and had based themselves in Chicago to be close to the originators of the music.

However, Johnny didn't stay in Chicago too long, returning to Texas, where he joined a jazz band formed by his brother Edgar. Johnny insisted on playing the blues, however, which wasn't the most popular form of music around at that time. In 1969 a small Texas record company, Sonobeat, heard about Johnny's extraordinary playing, and decided to record him at a ballroom in Austin, Texas, known as The Vulcan Gas Company. The resulting album *The Progressive Blues Experiment*, sold fairly well, and soon afterwards, *Rolling Stone* mentioned Johnny, who had meanwhile gone to check out the blues scene in Britain.

Johnny's manager, Steve Paul, signed him with Columbia (CBS) Records, while Liberty/United Artists had purchased the Sonobeat LP, so that there were two Johnny Winter albums released around the same time in mid-1969. The Columbia LP, simply titled *Johnny Winter*, was a fine complement to its Sonobeat brother. There was a great deal of interest in Johnny, which also was reflected in a renewed interest in the blues. However, a 'transitional' LP, *Second Winter*, also included several rock'n'roll cuts, and after the somewhat austere approach adopted earlier, it proved that Johnny could rock out with the best of his contemporaries.

The next step was to acquire a new band who could more easily cope with this change of direction, and Steve Paul came up with the idea of hiring the McCoys, who had scored a hit record some years before with *Hang on Sloopy*, but had somehow got lost in the psychedelic shuffle of the late 'sixties. Apart from their musical abilities, the great advantage of hiring the McCoys was that their leader Rick Derringer, being a top flight guitarist and singer, was able to share the band's front man duties, thus taking some of the load away from Johnny. This band were known as 'Johnny Winter And', and during 1971, after two successful albums, it seemed that finally Winter had found himself the perfect backing group.

Too late however. Pressure of life on the road had taken its toll on Johnny Winter and by the end of 1971, he was a drug addict, finally forcing himself to enter hospital voluntarily. He spent a painful period there of more than a year, after which he pronounced himself cured of his addiction. Not wanting to become involved in that same syndrome, Johnny eased himself back into music with another fine album, pointedly titled *Still Alive And Well*, which was released in 1973. He also began to tour again, but in very short bursts, and even four years later, there was still a feeling that he was holding back.

Edgar Winter and Rick Derringer continued to help Johnny on his gradual climb back to perfect health. While Johnny relied to some extent on a reputation gained before his addiction, albums like *Together*, a collection of rock'n'roll standards which he played with Edgar, began to indicate that he was again approaching top form and a proportion of his once vast audience started to take a renewed interest in his work.

Johnny Winter's first love in guitars is either a Gibson Thunderbird or the rather more photogenic Gibson Flying V, while for bottleneck work, for which he is justly rated among the best in the world, he uses a Fender 12-string with only six strings on it. He also uses a Fender Telecaster, but perhaps his most famous instrument is the steel National guitar pictured on the sleeve of *The Progressive Blues Experiment*.

Representative albums

The Progressive Blues Experiment *(Imperial/Sunset)*

Johnny Winter *(Columbia/CBS)*

Second Winter *(Columbia/CBS)*

Johnny Winter And *(Columbia/CBS)*

Still Alive and Well *(Columbia/CBS)*

Together *(Blue Sky)*

Johnny Winter, native of the State of Texas, is one of the best American blues guitarists.

Pictures supplied by:

Laurie Asprey: Endpapers, 34, 75; John Beecher: 14 (below), 15; Elaine Bryant/LFI Ltd: 64-5; Paul Canty/LFI Ltd: 19, 29, 80-81: Capitol Records: 20-21, 21; Dark Horse: 33; Chalkie Davies/WEA: 76; Simon Fowler/LFI Ltd: 48-9; LFI Ltd: 4, 13, 17, 31, 42, 46, 58, 88; Barry Levine/LFI Ltd: 71; Terry Lott/LFI Ltd: 83; Mercury Records: 51; New Musical Express: 1. 14 (top); 84-5; Popperfoto: 36, 39; Michael Putland/LFI Ltd: 2-3, 24-5, 40-41, 45, 52-3, 56-7, 66, 69; Michael Putland/WEA: 43; SKR Photos/LFI Ltd: 6; Tom Sheehan/CBS: 61, 62; Swan Song: 54; John Tobler: 10, 73; United Artists: 11; Virgin Records: 22; WEA: 9, 70, 78, 79, 86.